James B. Comey:

TESTIMONY

Former Federal Bureau of Investigation Director
Testifies regarding President Donald J. Trump before the
United States Senate Select Committee on Intelligence

Including
Full Statement for the Record
&
Public Testimony

WALKING C
CARNIVAL

Contents

Preface:

Press Release
Friday, May 19, 2017

Former FBI Director Comey Agrees to Testify in Open Session at Senate Intel Committee

Press Contact:
Becca Glover (Burr) 202-228-1616
Rachel Cohen (Warner) 202-228-6884

Friday, May 19, 2017
Former FBI Director Comey Agrees to Testify in Open Session at Senate Intel Committee

WASHINGTON –Senator Richard Burr (R-NC), Chairman of the Senate Select Committee on Intelligence, and Senator Mark Warner (D-VA), Vice Chairman of the Senate Select Committee on Intelligence, today announced that former Federal Bureau of Investigation Director James Comey has committed to testify in open session before the Committee. The Committee will schedule the open hearing after Memorial Day.

"The Committee looks forward to receiving testimony from the former Director on his role in the development of the Intelligence Community Assessment on Russian interference in the 2016 US elections, and I am hopeful that he will clarify for the American people recent events that have been broadly reported in the media," said Senator Burr.

"I hope that former Director Comey's testimony will help answer some of the questions that have arisen since Director Comey was so suddenly dismissed by the President. I also expect that Director Comey will be able to shed light on issues critical to this Committee's investigation of Russian interference in the 2016 election," said Senator Warner. "Director Comey served his country with honor for many years, and he deserves an opportunity to tell his story. Moreover, the American people deserve an opportunity to hear it."

###

Part One:

Statement for the Record

to the United States
Senate Select Committee on Intelligence

June 8, 2017

Presented to:

Chairman Richard Burr (R-North Carolina)
Ranking Member Mark Warner (D-Virginia)
Members of the Committee

Republicans

James Risch (Idaho)
Marco Rubio (Florida)
Susan Collins (Maine)
Roy Blunt (Missouri)
James Lankford (Oklahoma)
Tom Cotton (Arkansas)
John Cornyn (Texas)

Democrats

Dianne Feinstein (California)
Ron Wyden (Oregon)
Martin Heinrich (New Mexico)
Angus King (Maine)
Joe Manchin (West Virginia)
Kamala Harris (California)

Statement Text

Chairman Burr, Ranking Member Warner, Members of the Committee.

Thank you for inviting me to appear before you today. I was asked to testify today to describe for you my interactions with President-Elect and President Trump on subjects that I understand are of interest to you. I have not included every detail from my conversations with the President, but, to the best of my recollection, I have tried to include information that may be relevant to the Committee.

January 6 Briefing

I first met then-President-Elect Trump on Friday, January 6 in a conference room at Trump Tower in New York. I was there with other Intelligence Community (IC) leaders to brief him and his new national security team on the findings of an IC assessment concerning Russian efforts to interfere in the election. At the conclusion of that briefing, I remained alone with the President-Elect to brief him on some personally sensitive aspects of the information assembled during the assessment.

The IC leadership thought it important, for a variety of reasons, to alert the incoming President to the existence of this material, even though it was salacious and unverified. Among those reasons were: (1) we knew the media was about to publicly report the material and we believed the IC should not keep knowledge of the material and its imminent release from the President-Elect; and (2) to the extent there was some effort to compromise an incoming President, we could blunt any such effort with a defensive briefing.

The Director of National Intelligence asked that I personally do this portion of the briefing because I was staying in my position and because the material implicated the FBI's counter-intelligence responsibilities. We also agreed I would do it alone to minimize potential embarrassment to the President-Elect. Although we agreed it made sense for me to do the briefing, the FBI's leadership and I were concerned that the briefing might create a situation where a new President came into office uncertain about whether the FBI was conducting a counter-intelligence investigation of his personal conduct.

It is important to understand that FBI counter-intelligence investigations are different than the more-commonly known criminal investigative work. The Bureau's goal in a counter-intelligence investigation is to understand the technical and human methods that hostile foreign powers are using to influence the United States or to steal our secrets. The FBI uses that understanding to disrupt those efforts. Sometimes disruption takes the form of alerting a person who is targeted for recruitment or influence by the foreign power. Sometimes it involves hardening a computer system that is being attacked. Sometimes it involves "turning" the recruited person into a double-agent, or publicly calling out the behavior with sanctions or expulsions of embassy-based intelligence officers. On occasion, criminal prosecution is used to disrupt intelligence activities.

Because the nature of the hostile foreign nation is well known, counterintelligence investigations tend to be centered on individuals the FBI suspects to be witting or unwitting agents of that foreign power. When the FBI develops reason to believe an American has been targeted for recruitment by a foreign power or is covertly acting as an agent of the foreign power, the FBI will "open an investigation" on that American and use legal authorities to try to learn more about the nature of any relationship with the foreign power so it can be disrupted.

In that context, prior to the January 6 meeting, I discussed with the FBI's leadership team whether I should be prepared to assure President-Elect Trump that we were not investigating him personally. That was true; we did not have an open counter-intelligence case on him. We agreed I should do so if circumstances warranted. During our one-on-one meeting at Trump Tower, based on President-Elect Trump's reaction to the briefing and without him directly asking the question, I offered that assurance.

I felt compelled to document my first conversation with the President-Elect in a memo. To ensure accuracy, I began to type it on a laptop in an FBI vehicle outside Trump Tower the moment I walked out of the meeting. Creating written records immediately after one-on-one conversations with Mr. Trump was my practice from that point forward. This had not been my practice in the past. I spoke alone with President Obama twice in person (and never on the phone) – once in 2015 to discuss law enforcement policy issues and a second time, briefly, for him to say goodbye in late 2016. In neither of those circumstances did I memorialize the discussions. I can recall nine one-on-one conversations with President Trump in four months – three in person and six on the phone.

January 27 Dinner

The President and I had dinner on Friday, January 27 at 6:30 pm in the Green Room at the White House. He had called me at lunchtime that day and invited me to dinner that night, saying he was going to invite my whole family, but decided to have just me this time, with the whole family coming the next time. It was unclear from the conversation who else would be at the dinner, although I assumed there would be others.

It turned out to be just the two of us, seated at a small oval table in the center of the Green Room. Two Navy stewards waited on us, only entering the room to serve food and drinks.

The President began by asking me whether I wanted to stay on as FBI Director, which I found strange because he had already told me twice in earlier conversations that he hoped I would stay, and I had assured him that I intended to. He said that lots of people wanted my job and, given the abuse I had taken during the previous year, he would understand if I wanted to walk away.

My instincts told me that the one-on-one setting, and the pretense that this was our first discussion about my position, meant the dinner was, at least in part, an effort to have me ask for my job and create some sort of patronage relationship. That concerned me greatly, given the FBI's traditionally independent status in the executive branch.

I replied that I loved my work and intended to stay and serve out my ten-year term as Director. And then, because the set-up made me uneasy, I added that I was not "reliable" in the way politicians use that word, but he could always count on me to tell him the truth. I added that I was not on anybody's side politically and could not be counted on in the traditional political sense, a stance I said was in his best interest as the President.

A few moments later, the President said, "I need loyalty, I expect loyalty." I didn't move, speak, or change my facial expression in any way during the awkward silence that followed. We simply looked at each other in silence. The conversation then moved on, but he returned to the subject near the end of our dinner.

At one point, I explained why it was so important that the FBI and the Department of Justice be independent of the White House. I said it was a paradox: Throughout history, some Presidents have decided that because "problems" come from Justice, they should try to hold the Department close. But blurring those boundaries ultimately makes the problems worse by undermining public trust in the institutions and their work.

Near the end of our dinner, the President returned to the subject of my job, saying he was very glad I wanted to stay, adding that he had heard great things about me from Jim Mattis, Jeff Sessions, and many others. He then said, "I need loyalty." I replied, "You will always get honesty from me." He paused and then said, "That's what I want, honest loyalty." I paused, and then said, "You will get that from me." As I wrote in the memo I created immediately after the dinner, it is possible we understood the phrase "honest loyalty" differently, but I decided it wouldn't be productive to push it further. The term – honest loyalty – had helped end a very awkward conversation and my explanations had made clear what he should expect.

During the dinner, the President returned to the salacious material I had briefed him about on January 6, and, as he had done previously, expressed his disgust for the allegations and strongly denied them. He said he was considering ordering me to investigate the alleged incident to prove it didn't happen. I replied that he should give that careful thought because it might create a narrative that we were investigating him personally, which we weren't, and because it was very difficult to prove a negative. He said he would think about it and asked me to think about it.

As was my practice for conversations with President Trump, I wrote a detailed memo about the dinner immediately afterwards and shared it with the senior leadership team of the FBI.

February 14 Oval Office Meeting

On February 14, I went to the Oval Office for a scheduled counterterrorism briefing of the President. He sat behind the desk and a group of us sat in a semi-circle of about six chairs facing him on the other side of the desk. The Vice President, Deputy Director of the CIA, Director of the National Counter-Terrorism Center, Secretary of Homeland Security, the Attorney General, and I were in the semi-circle of chairs. I was directly facing the President, sitting between the Deputy CIA Director and the Director of NCTC. There were quite a few others in the room, sitting behind us on couches and chairs.

The President signaled the end of the briefing by thanking the group and telling them all that he wanted to speak to me alone. I stayed in my chair. As the participants started to leave the Oval Office, the Attorney General lingered by my chair, but the President thanked him and said he wanted to speak only with me. The last person to leave was Jared Kushner, who also stood by my chair and exchanged pleasantries with me. The President then excused him, saying he wanted to speak with me.

When the door by the grandfather clock closed, and we were alone, the President began by saying, "I want to talk about Mike Flynn." Flynn had resigned the previous day. The President began by saying Flynn hadn't done anything wrong in speaking with the Russians, but he had to let him go because he had misled the Vice President. He added that he had other concerns about Flynn, which he did not then specify.

The President then made a long series of comments about the problem with leaks of classified information – a concern I shared and still share. After he had spoken for a few minutes about leaks, Reince Priebus leaned in through the door by the grandfather clock and I could see a group of people waiting behind him. The President waved at him to close the door, saying he would be done shortly. The door closed.

The President then returned to the topic of Mike Flynn, saying, "He is a good guy and has been through a lot." He repeated that Flynn hadn't done anything wrong on his calls with the Russians, but had misled the Vice President. He then said, "I hope you can see your way clear to letting this go, to letting Flynn go. He is a good guy. I hope you can let this go." I replied only that "he is a good guy." (In fact, I had a positive experience dealing with Mike Flynn when he was a colleague as Director of the Defense Intelligence Agency at the beginning of my term at FBI.) I did not say I would "let this go."

The President returned briefly to the problem of leaks. I then got up and left out the door by the grandfather clock, making my way through the large group of people waiting there, including Mr. Priebus and the Vice President.

15

I immediately prepared an unclassified memo of the conversation about Flynn and discussed the matter with FBI senior leadership. I had understood the President to be requesting that we drop any investigation of Flynn in connection with false statements about his conversations with the Russian ambassador in December. I did not understand the President to be talking about the broader investigation into Russia or possible links to his campaign. I could be wrong, but I took him to be focusing on what had just happened with Flynn's departure and the controversy around his account of his phone calls. Regardless, it was very concerning, given the FBI's role as an independent investigative agency.

The FBI leadership team agreed with me that it was important not to infect the investigative team with the President's request, which we did not intend to abide. We also concluded that, given that it was a one-on-one conversation, there was nothing available to corroborate my account. We concluded it made little sense to report it to Attorney General Sessions, who we expected would likely recuse himself from involvement in Russia-related investigations. (He did so two weeks later.) The Deputy Attorney General's role was then filled in an acting capacity by a United States Attorney, who would also not be long in the role. After discussing the matter, we decided to keep it very closely held, resolving to figure out what to do with it down the road as our investigation progressed. The investigation moved ahead at full speed, with none of the investigative team members – or the Department of Justice lawyers supporting them – aware of the President's request.

Shortly afterwards, I spoke with Attorney General Sessions in person to pass along the President's concerns about leaks. I took the opportunity to implore the Attorney General to prevent any future direct communication between the President and me. I told the AG that what had just happened – him being asked to leave while the FBI Director, who reports to the AG, remained behind – was inappropriate and should never happen. He did not reply. For the reasons discussed above, I did not mention that the President broached the FBI's potential investigation of General Flynn.

March 30 Phone Call

On the morning of March 30, the President called me at the FBI. He described the Russia investigation as "a cloud" that was impairing his ability to act on behalf of the country. He said he had nothing to do with Russia, had not been involved with hookers in Russia, and had always assumed he was being recorded when in Russia. He asked what we could do to "lift the cloud." I responded that we were investigating the matter as quickly as we could, and that there would be great benefit, if we didn't find anything, to our having done the work well. He agreed, but then re-emphasized the problems this was causing him.

Then the President asked why there had been a congressional hearing about Russia the previous week – at which I had, as the Department of Justice directed, confirmed the investigation into possible coordination between Russia and the Trump campaign. I explained the demands from the leadership of both parties in Congress for more information, and that Senator Grassley had even held up the confirmation of the Deputy Attorney General until we briefed him in detail on the investigation. I explained that we had briefed the leadership of Congress on exactly which individuals we were investigating and that we had told those Congressional leaders that we were not personally investigating President Trump. I reminded him I had previously told him that. He repeatedly told me, "We need to get that fact out." (I did not tell the President that the FBI and the Department of Justice had been reluctant to make public statements that we did not have an open case on President Trump for a number of reasons, most importantly because it would create a duty to correct, should that change.)

The President went on to say that if there were some "satellite" associates of his who did something wrong, it would be good to find that out, but that he hadn't done anything wrong and hoped I would find a way to get it out that we weren't investigating him.

In an abrupt shift, he turned the conversation to FBI Deputy Director Andrew McCabe, saying he hadn't brought up "the McCabe thing" because I had said McCabe was honorable, although McAuliffe was close to the Clintons and had given him (I think he meant Deputy Director McCabe's wife) campaign money. Although I didn't understand why the President was bringing this up, I repeated that Mr. McCabe was an honorable person.

He finished by stressing "the cloud" that was interfering with his ability to make deals for the country and said he hoped I could find a way to get out that he wasn't being investigated. I told him I would see what we could do, and that we would do our investigative work well and as quickly as we could.

Immediately after that conversation, I called Acting Deputy Attorney General Dana Boente (AG Sessions had by then recused himself on all Russia-related matters), to report the substance of the call from the President, and said I would await his guidance. I did not hear back from him before the President called me again two weeks later.

April 11 Phone Call

On the morning of April 11, the President called me and asked what I had done about his request that I "get out" that he is not personally under investigation. I replied that I had passed his request to the Acting Deputy Attorney General, but I had not heard back. He replied that "the cloud" was getting in the way of his ability to do his job. He said that perhaps he would have his people reach out to the Acting Deputy Attorney General. I said that was the way his request should be handled. I said the White House Counsel should contact the leadership of DOJ to make the request, which was the traditional channel.

He said he would do that and added, "Because I have been very loyal to you, very loyal; we had that thing you know." I did not reply or ask him what he meant by "that thing." I said only that the way to handle it was to have the White House Counsel call the Acting Deputy Attorney General. He said that was what he would do and the call ended.

That was the last time I spoke with President Trump.

Part Two:

June 8, 2017
Public Testimony

before the United States
Senate Select Committee on Intelligence

Transcript: Senate Testimony

CHAIRMAN RICHARD BURR: I'd like to call this hearing to order.

Director Comey, I appreciate your willingness to appear before the committee today, and more importantly, I thank you for your dedicated service and leadership to the Federal Bureau of Investigation. Your appearance today speaks to the trust we have built over the years, and I'm looking forward to a very open and candid discussion today.

I'd like to remind my colleagues that we will reconvene in closed session at 1 PM today and I ask that you reserve for that venue any questions that might get into classified information. The director has been very gracious with his time, but the vice chairman and I have worked out a very specific timeline for his commitment to be on the Hill, so we will do everything we can to meet that agreement.

The Senate Select Committee on Intelligence exists to certify for the other 85 members of the United States Senate and the American people that the intelligence community is operating lawfully and has the necessary authorities and tools to accomplish its mission and keep America safe. Part of our mission, beyond the oversight we continue to provide to the intelligence community and its activities, is to investigate Russian interference in the 2016 U.S. elections. The committee's work continues. This hearing represents part of that effort.

Jim, allegations have been swirling in the press for the last several weeks, and today's your opportunity to set the record straight. Yesterday, I read with interest your statement for the record. And I think it provides some helpful details surrounding your interactions with the president.

It clearly lays out your understanding of those discussions, actions you took following each conversation and your state of mind. I very much appreciate your candor, and I think it's helpful as we work through to determine the ultimate truth behind possible Russian interference in the 2016 elections.

Your statement also provides texture and context to your interactions with the president, from your vantage point, and outlines a strained relationship. The American people need to hear your side of the story just as they need to hear the president's descriptions of events.

These interactions also highlight the importance of the committee's ongoing investigation. Our experienced staff is interviewing all relevant parties and some of the most sensitive intelligence in our country's possession.

We will establish the facts, separate from rampant speculation, and lay them out for the American people to make their own judgment. Only then will we as a nation be able to move forward and to put this episode to rest. There are several outstanding issues not addressed in your statement that I hope you'll clear up for the American people today. Did the president's request for loyalty — your impression that — that the one-on-one dinner of January 27th was, and I quote, "at least in part an effort to create some sort of patronage relationship," or his March 30th phone call asking what you could do to lift the cloud of Russia investigation in any way, alter your approach of the FBI's investigation into General Flynn or the broader investigation into Russia and possible links to the campaign?

In your opinion, did potential Russian efforts to establish links with individuals in the Trump orbit rise to the level we could define as collusion? Or was it a counterintelligence concern?

There's been a significant public speculation about your decision-making related to the Clinton e-mail investigation. Why did you decide publicly — to publicly announce FBI's recommendations that the Department of Justice not pursue criminal charges? You have described it as a choice between a bad decision and a worse decision. The American people need to understand the facts behind your action.

This committee is uniquely suited to investigate Russia's interference in the 2016 elections. We also have a unified, bipartisan approach to what is a highly charged partisan issue. Russian activities during 2016 election may have been aimed at one party's candidate, but as my colleague, Senator Rubio, says frequently, in 2018 and 2020, it could be aimed at anyone, at home or abroad.

My colleague, Senator Warner, and I have worked in — have worked to stay in lockstep on this investigation. We've had our differences on approach at times. But I've constantly stressed that we need to be a team. And I think Senator Warner agrees with me.

We must keep these questions above politics and partisanship. It's too important to be tainted by anyone trying to score political points.

With that, again, I welcome you, Director. And I turn to the vice chairman for any comments he might have.

SENATOR MARK WARNER: Well, thank you, Mr. Chairman.

And let me start by, again, absolutely thanking all the members of the committee for the seriousness in which they've taken on this task.

Mr. Comey, thank you for agreeing to come testify as part of this committee's investigation into Russia. I realize that this hearing has been, obviously, the focus of a lot of Washington in the last few days. But the truth is many Americans who may be tuning in today probably haven't focused on every twist and turn of the investigation.

So I'd like to briefly describe, at least from this senator's standpoint, what we already know and what we're still investigating. To be clear, this whole investigation is not about re-litigating the election. It's not about who won or lost. And it sure as heck is not about Democrats versus Republicans.

We're here because a foreign adversary attacked us right here at home, plain and simple, not by guns or missiles, but by foreign operatives seeking to hijack our most important democratic process — our presidential election.

Russian spies engaged in a series of online cyber raids and a broad campaign of disinformation, all ultimately aimed at sowing chaos to us to undermine public faith in our process, in our leadership and ultimately in ourselves.

And that's not just this senator's opinion, it is the unanimous determination of the entire U.S. intelligence community. So we must find out the full story, what the Russians did, and, candidly, as some other colleagues have mentioned, why they were so successful. And, more importantly, we must determine the necessary steps to take to protect our democracy and ensure they can't do it again.

Chairman mentioned elections in 2018 and 2020. In my home state of Virginia, we have elections this year, in 2017. Simply put, we cannot let anything or anyone prevent us from getting to the bottom of this.

Now, Mr. Comey, let me say at the outset we haven't always agreed on every issue. In fact, I've occasionally questioned some of the actions you've taken. But I've never had any reason to question your integrity, your expertise or your intelligence.

You've been a straight shooter with this committee, and have been willing to speak truth to power, even at the risk of your own career, which makes the way in which you were fired by the president ultimately shocking.

Recall, we began this entire process with the president and his staff first denying that the Russians were ever involved, and then falsely claiming that no one from his team was never in touch with any Russians.

We know that's just not the truth. Numerous Trump associates had undisclosed contacts with Russians before and after the election, including the president's attorney general, his former national security adviser and his current senior adviser, Mr. Kushner.

That doesn't even begin to count the host of additional campaign associates and advisers who've also been caught up in this massive web. We saw Mr. Trump's campaign manager, Mr. Manafort, forced to step down over ties to Russian-backed entities. The national security adviser, General Flynn, had to resign over his lies about engagements with the Russians.

And we saw the candidate him — himself, express an odd and unexplained affection for the Russian dictator, while calling for the hacking of his opponent. There's a lot to investigate. Enough, in fact that then Director Comey publicly acknowledged that he was leading an investigation into those links between Mr. Trump's campaign and the Russian government.

As the director of the FBI, Mr. Comey was ultimately responsible for conducting that investigation, which might explain why you're sitting now as a private citizen.

What we didn't know was, at the same time that this investigation was proceeding, the president himself appears to have been engaged in an effort to influence, or at least co-opt, the director of the FBI. The testimony that Mr. Comey has submitted for today's hearing is very disturbing.

For example, on January 27th, after summoning Director Comey to dinner, the president appears to have threatened the director's job while telling him, quote, "I need loyalty. I expect loyalty."

At a later meeting, on February 14th, the president asked the attorney general to leave the Oval Office so that he could privately ask Director Comey, again, quote, "to see way clear to letting Flynn go."

That is a statement that Director Comey interpreted as a — as a request that he drop the investigation, connected to General Flynn's false statements. Think about it: the president of the United States asking the FBI director to drop an ongoing investigation.

And, after that, the president called the FBI director on two additional occasions, March 30th and April 11th, and asked him again, quote, "to lift the cloud" on the Russian investigation.

Now, Director Comey denied each of these improper requests. The loyalty pledge, the admonition to drop the Flynn investigation, the request to lift the cloud on the Russia investigation. Of course, after his refusals, Director Comey was fired.

The initial explanation for the firing didn't pass any smell test. So now Director Comey was fired because he didn't treat Hillary Clinton appropriately. Of course, that explanation lasted about a day, because the president himself then made very clear that he was thinking about Russia when he decided to fire Director Comey.

Shockingly, reports suggest that the president admitted as much in an Oval Office meeting with the Russians the day after Director Comey was fired, disparaging our country's top law enforcement official as a, quote/unquote, "nut job." The president allegedly suggested that his firing relieved great pressure on his feelings about Russia.

This is not happening in isolation. At the same time the president was engaged in these efforts with Director Comey, he was also, at least allegedly, asking senior leaders of the intelligence community to downplay the Russia investigation or to intervene with the director.

Yesterday, we had DNI Director Coats and NSA Director Admiral Rogers, who were offered a number of opportunities to flatly deny those press reports. They expressed their opinions, but they did not take that opportunity to deny those reports. They did not take advantage of that opportunity. In my belief, that's not how the president of the United States should behave.

Regardless of the outcome of our investigation into the Russia links, Director Comey's firing and his testimony raise separate and troubling questions that we must get to the bottom of.

Again, as I said at the outset, I've seen firsthand how seriously every member of this committee is taking his work. I'm proud of the committee's efforts so far. Let me be clear: This is not a witch hunt. This is not fake news. It is an effort to protect our country from a new threat that, quite honestly, will not go away any time soon.

So, Mr. Comey, your testimony here today will help us move towards that goal. I look forward to that testimony.

WARNER: Thank you, Mr. Chairman.

BURR: Thank you, Vice Chairman.

Director, as discussed, when you agreed to appear before the committee, it would be under oath. I'd ask you to please stand. Raise your right hand. Do you solemnly swear to tell the truth, the whole truth, and nothing but the truth, so help you God?

COMEY: (OFF-MIKE)

BURR: Please be seated.

Director Comey, you're now under oath.

And I would just note to members, you will be recognized by seniority for a period up to seven minutes. And again, it is the intent to move to a closed session no later than 1 p.m.

With that, Director Comey, you are recognized. You have the floor for as long as you might need.

COMEY: Thank you, Mr. Chairman. Ranking Member Warner, members of the committee, thank you for inviting me here to testify today. I've submitted my statement for the record and I'm not going to repeat it here this morning. I thought I would just offer some very brief introductory remarks and then I would welcome your questions.

When I was appointed FBI director in 2013, I understood that I served at the pleasure of the president. Even though I was appointed to a 10 year term, which Congress created in order to underscore the importance of the FBI being outside of politics and independent, I understood that I could be fired by a president for any reason, or for no reason at all.

And on May the 9th, when I learned that I had been fired, for that reason, I immediately came home as a private citizen. But then, the explanations — the shifting explanations, confused me and increasingly concerned me.

They confused me because the president and I had had multiple conversations about my job, both before and after he took office. And he had repeatedly told me I was doing a great job and he hoped I would stay. And I had repeatedly assured him that I did intend to stay and serve out the remaining six years of my term.

He told me repeatedly that he had talked to lots of people about me, including our current attorney general, and had learned that I was doing a great job and that I was extremely well-liked by the FBI workforce.

So it confused me when I saw on television the president saying that he actually fired me because of the Russia investigation and learned, again, from the media that he was telling, privately, other parties that my firing had relieved great pressure on the Russia investigation.

I was also confused by the initial explanation that was offered publicly, that I was fired because of the decisions I had made during the election year. That didn't make sense to me for a whole bunch of reasons, including the time and all the water that had gone under the bridge since those hard decisions that had to be made. That didn't make any sense to me.

And although the law required no reason at all to fire an FBI director, the administration then chose to defame me and, more importantly, the FBI by saying that the organization was in disarray, that it was poorly led, that the workforce had lost confidence in its leader.

Those were lies, plain and simple, and I am so sorry that the FBI work-force had to hear them and I'm so sorry that the American people were told them.

I worked every day at the FBI to help make that great organization better. And I say "help" because I did nothing alone at the FBI. There are no indispensable people at the FBI. The organization's great strength is that its values and abilities run deep and wide.

The FBI will be fine without me. The FBI's mission will be relentlessly pursued by its people, and that mission is to protect the American people and uphold the Constitution of the United States.

I will deeply miss being part of that mission, but this organization and its mission will go on long beyond me and long beyond any particular administration.

I have a message before I close for the — my former colleagues at the FBI. But first, I want the American people to know this truth: The FBI is honest. The FBI is strong. And the FBI is, and always will be, inde-pendent.

And now to my former colleagues, if I may. I am so sorry that I didn't get the chance to say goodbye to you properly. It was the honor of my life to serve beside you, to be part of the FBI family. And I will miss it for the rest of my life.

Thank you for standing watch. Thank you for doing so much good for this country. Do that good as long as ever you can.

And, Senators, I look forward to your questions.

BURR: Director, thank you for that testimony, both oral and the written testimony that you provided to the committee yesterday and made public to the American people.

The chair would recognize himself, first, for 12 minutes, vice chair for 12 minutes, based upon the agreement we have.

Director, did the Special Counsel's Office review and/or edit your writ-ten testimony?

COMEY: No.

BURR: Do you have any doubt that Russia attempted to interfere in the 2016 elections?

COMEY: None.

BURR: Do you have any doubt that the Russian government was behind the intrusions in the DNC and the DCCC systems, and the subsequent leaks of that information?

COMEY: No, no doubt.

BURR: Do you have any doubt that the Russian government was behind the cyber intrusion in the state voter files?

COMEY: No.

BURR: Do you have any doubt that officials of the Russian government were fully aware of these activities?

COMEY: No doubt.

BURR: Are you confident that no votes cast in the 2016 presidential election were altered?

COMEY: I'm confident. By the time — when I left as director, I had seen no indication of that whatsoever.

BURR: Director Comey, did the president at any time ask you to stop the FBI investigation into Russian involvement in the 2016 U.S. elections?

COMEY: Not to my understanding, no.

BURR: Did any individual working for this administration, including the Justice Department, ask you to stop the Russian investigation?

COMEY: No.

BURR: Director, when the president requested that you, and I quote, "let Flynn go," General Flynn had an unreported contact with the Russians, which is an offense. And if press accounts are right, there might have been discrepancies between facts and his FBI testimony.

In your estimation, was General Flynn, at that time, in serious legal jeopardy? And in addition to that, do you sense that the president was trying to obstruct justice, or just seek for a way for Mike Flynn to save face, given he had already been fired?

COMEY: General Flynn, at that point in time, was in legal jeopardy. There was an open FBI criminal investigation of his statements in connection with the Russian contacts and the contacts themselves. And so that was my assessment at the time.

I don't think it's for me to say whether the conversation I had with the president was an effort to obstruct. I took it as a very disturbing thing, very concerning, but that's a conclusion I'm sure the special counsel will work towards, to try and understand what the intention was there, and whether that's an offense.

BURR: Director, is it possible that, as part of this FBI investigation, the FBI could find evidence of criminality that is not tied to — to the 2016 elections — possible collusion or coordination with Russians?

COMEY: Sure.

BURR: So there could be something that just fits a criminal aspect to this that doesn't have anything to do with the 2016 election cycle?

COMEY: Correct. In any complex investigation, when you start turning over rocks, sometimes you find things that are unrelated to the primary investigation, that are criminal in nature.

BURR: Director Comey, you have been criticized publicly for the decision to present your findings on the e-mail investigation directly to the American people. Have you learned anything since that time that would've changed what you said, or how you chose to inform the American people?

COMEY: Honestly, no. I mean, it caused a whole lot of personal pain for me, but, as I look back, given what I knew at the time and even what I've learned since, I think it was the best way to try and protect the justice institution, including the FBI.

BURR: In the public domain is this question of the Steele dossier, a document that has been around, now, for over a year. I'm not sure when the FBI first took possession of it, but the media had it before you had it and we had it. At the time of your departure from the FBI, was the FBI able to confirm any criminal allegations contained in the Steele document?

COMEY: Mr. Chairman, I don't think that's a question I can answer in an open setting because it goes into the details of the investigation.

BURR: Director, the term we hear most often is "collusion." When people are describing possible links between Americans and Russian government entities related to the interference in our election, would you say that it's normal for foreign governments to reach out to members of an incoming administration?

COMEY: Yes.

BURR: At what point does the normal contact cross the line into an attempt to recruit agents or influence or spies?

COMEY: Difficult to say in the abstract. It depends upon the context, whether there's an effort to keep it covert, what the nature of the requests made of the American by the foreign government are. It's a — it's a judgment call based on a whole lot of facts.

BURR: At what point would that recruitment become a counterintelligence threat to our country?

COMEY: Again, difficult to answer in the abstract. But when — when a foreign power is using especially coercion or some sort of pressure to try and co-opt an American, especially a government official, to act on its behalf, that's a serious concern to the FBI and at the heart of the FBI's counterintelligence mission.

BURR: So if you've got a — a — a 36-page document of — of specific claims that are out there, the FBI would have to, for counterintelligence reasons, try to verify anything that might be claimed in there. One, and probably first and foremost, is the counterintelligence concerns that we have about blackmail. Would that be an accurate statement?

COMEY: Yes. If the FBI receives a credible allegation that there is some effort to co-opt, coerce, direct, employ covertly an American on behalf of the foreign power, that's the basis on which a counterintelligence investigation is opened.

BURR: And when you read the dossier, what was your reaction, given that it was 100 percent directed at the president-elect?

COMEY: Not a question I can answer in an open setting, Mr. Chairman.

BURR: OK. When did you become aware of the cyber intrusion?

COMEY: The first cyber — it was all kinds of cyber intrusions going on all the time. The first Russia-connected cyber intrusion, I became aware of in the late summer of 2015.

BURR: And in that time frame, there were more than the DNC and the DCCC that were targets.

COMEY: Correct. There was a massive effort to target government and nongovernmental — near-governmental agencies like nonprofits.

BURR: What would be the estimate of how many entities out there the Russians specifically targeted in that time frame?

COMEY: It's hundreds. I suppose it could be more than 1,000, but it's at least hundreds.

BURR: When did you become aware that data had been exfiltrated?

COMEY: I'm not sure, exactly. I think either late '15 or early '16.

BURR: And did — did you, the director of the FBI, have conversations with the last administration about the risk that this posed?

COMEY: Yes.

BURR: And share with us, if you will, what actions they took.

COMEY: Well, the FBI had already undertaken an effort to notify all the victims — and that's what we consider the entities that were attacked as part of this massive spear phishing campaign. And so we notified them in an effort to disrupt what might be ongoing.

Then there was a series of continuing interactions with entities through the rest of '15 into '16, and then, throughout '16, the administration was trying to decide how to respond to the intrusion activity that it saw.

BURR: And the FBI, in this case, unlike other cases that you might investigate — did you ever have access to the actual hardware that was hacked? Or did you have to rely on a third party to provide you the data that they had collected?

COMEY: In the case of the DNC, and, I believe, the DCCC, but I'm sure the DNC, we did not have access to the devices themselves. We got relevant forensic information from a private party, a high-class entity, that had done the work. But we didn't get direct access.

BURR: But no content?

COMEY: Correct.

BURR: Isn't content an important part of the forensics from a counterintelligence standpoint?

COMEY: It is, although what was briefed to me by my folks — the people who were my folks at the time is that they had gotten the information from the private party that they needed to understand the intrusion by the spring of 2016.BURR: Let me go back, if I can, very briefly, to the decision to publicly go out with your results on the e-mail.

Was your decision influenced by the attorney general's tarmac meeting with the former president, Bill Clinton?

COMEY: Yes. In — in an ultimately conclusive way, that was the thing that capped it for me, that I had to do something separately to protect the credibility of the investigation, which meant both the FBI and the Justice Department.

BURR: Were there other things that contributed to that that you can describe in an open session?

COMEY: There were other things that contributed to that. One significant item I can't, I know the committee's been briefed on. There's been some public accounts of it, which are nonsense, but I understand the committee's been briefed on the classified facts.

Probably the only other consideration that I guess I can talk about in an open setting is, at one point, the attorney general had directed me not to call it an investigation, but instead to call it a matter, which confused me and concerned me.

But that was one of the bricks in the load that led me to conclude, I have to step away from the department if we're to close this case credibly.

BURR: Director, my last question: You're not only a seasoned prosecutor, you've led the FBI for years. You understand the investigative process. You've worked with this committee closely, and we're grateful to you because I think we've — we've mutually built trust in what your organization does and — and what we do.

Is there any doubt in your mind that this committee can carry out its oversight role in the 2016 Russian involvement in the elections in parallel with the — now — special counsel that's been set up?

COMEY: No — no doubt. It can be done. It requires lots of conversations, but Bob Mueller is one of this country's great, great pros. And I'm sure you all will be able to work it out with him to run it in parallel.

BURR: I want to thank you once again, and I want to turn to the vice chairman.

WARNER: Thank you, Mr. Chairman. And, again, Director Comey, thank you for your service.

And your comments to your FBI family, I know, were heartfelt. Know that, even though there are some in the administration who've tried to smear your reputation, you had Acting Director McCabe, in public testimony a few weeks back and in public testimony yesterday, reaffirm that the vast majority of the FBI community had great trust in your leadership and, obviously, trust in your integrity.

I want to go through a number of the meetings that you referenced in your testimony. And let's start with the January 6th meeting in Trump Tower, where you went up with a series of officials to brief the president-elect on the Russia investigation. My understanding is you remained afterwards to brief him on, again, quote, "some personally sensitive aspects" of the information you relayed.

Now, you said, after that briefing, you felt compelled to document that conversation, that you actually started documenting it soon as you got into the car.

Now, you've had extensive experience at the Department of Justice and at the FBI. You've worked under presidents of both parties. What was it about that meeting that led you to determine that you needed to start putting down a written record?

COMEY: A combination of things, I think — the circumstances, the subject matter and the person I was interacting with. Circumstances first: I was alone with the president of the United States — or the president-elect, soon to be president.

The subject matter: I was talking about matters that touch on the FBI's core responsibility and that relate to the president — president-elect personally.

And then the nature of the person: I was honestly concerned that he might lie about the nature of our meeting, and so I thought it really important to document.

That combination of things, I'd never experienced before, but it led me to believe I've got to write it down, and I've got to write it down in a very detailed way.

WARNER: I think that's a very important statement you just made. And my understanding is that then, again, unlike your dealings with presidents of either parties in your past experience, in every subsequent meeting or conversation with this president, you created a written record.

Did you feel that you needed to create this written record or these memos because they might need to be relied on at some future date?

COMEY: Sure. I created records after conversations, and I think I did it after each of our nine conversations. If I didn't, I did it for nearly all of them, especially the ones that were substantive.

I knew that there might come a day when I would need a record of what had happened, not just to defend myself, but to defend the FBI and — and our integrity as an institution and the independence of our investigative function. That's what made this so — so difficult, is it was a combination of circumstances, subject matter, and the particular person.

WARNER: And so, in all your experience, this was the only president that you felt like, in every meeting, you needed to document, because at some point, using your words, he might put out a non-truthful representation of that meeting?

Now...

(CROSSTALK)

COMEY: That's right, Senator.

And I — I — as I said in my written testimony, as FBI director, I interacted with President Obama. I spoke only twice in three years, and didn't document it. When I was deputy attorney general, I had one one-on-one meeting with President Bush about a very important and difficult national security matter.

I didn't write a memo documenting that conversation either — sent a quick e-mail to my staff to let them know there was something going on, but I didn't feel, with President Bush, the need to document it in that way, again, because of — the combination of those factors just wasn't present with either President Bush or President Obama.

WARNER: I — I think that is very significant. I think others will probably question that.

Now, our chairman and I have requested those memos. It is our hope that the FBI will get this committee access to those memos so that, again, we can read that contemporaneous rendition, so that we've got your side of the story.

Now, I know members have said, and press has said, that if you were — a great deal's been made of whether the president — you were asked to, in effect, indicate whether the president was the subject of any investigation.

And my understanding is, prior to your meeting on January 6th, you discussed with your leadership team whether or not you should be prepared to assure then President-Elect Trump that the FBI was not investigating him personally.

Now, my understanding is your leadership team agreed with that. But was that a unanimous decision? Was there any debate about that?

COMEY: Was it unanimous? One of the members of the leadership team had a view that, although it was technically true, we did not have a counterintelligence file case open on then-President-elect Trump.

His concern was, because we're looking at the potential — again, that's the subject of the investigation — coordination between the campaign and Russia, because it was President Trump — President-elect Trump's campaign, this person's view was, inevitably, his behavior, his conduct will fall within the scope of that work.

And so he was reluctant to make the statement that I made. I disagreed. I thought it was fair to say what was literally true: There is not a counterintelligence investigation of Mr. Trump. And I decided, in the moment, to say it, given the nature of our conversation.

WARNER: At that moment in time, did you ever revisit that as a — in — in these subsequent sessions?

COMEY: With the FBI leadership team?

WARNER: With the team — with your team.

COMEY: Sure, and — and the — the leader who had that view — it didn't change. His view was still that it was probably — although literally true, his concern was it could be misleading, because the nature of the investigation was such that it might well touch — obviously, it would touch the campaign, and the person at the head of the campaign would be the candidate. And so that was his view throughout.

WARNER: Let me move to the January 27th dinner, where you said, quote, "The president began by asking me whether I wanted to stay on as FBI director. He also indicated that lots of people" — again, your words — "wanted the job."

You go on to say that the dinner itself was seemingly an effort to, quote, "have you ask him for your job," and create some sort of, quote/unquote, "patronage relationship."

The president's — seems, from my reading of your memo, to be holding your job, or your possibility of continuing in your job, over your head in a fairly direct way. What was your impression, and what did you mean by this notion of a patronage relationship?

COMEY: Well, my impression — and, again, it's my impression. I could always be wrong. But my common sense told me that what was going on is either he had concluded, or someone had told him, that you didn't — you've already asked Comey to stay, and you didn't get anything for it, and that the dinner was an effort to build a relationship — in fact, he asked specifically — of loyalty in the context of asking me to stay.

And, as I said, what was odd about that is we'd already talked twice about it by that point. And he'd said, I very much hope you'll stay, I hope you'll stay.

In fact, I just remembered, sitting here, a third one. When — you've seen the picture of me walking across the Blue Room. And what the president whispered in my ear was, "I really look forward to working with you." So, after those encounters...

WARNER: And that was just a few days before you were fired.

COMEY:... yeah, that was on the 20 — the Sunday after the inauguration.

The next Friday, I have dinner, and the president begins by wanting to talk about my job. And so I'm sitting there, thinking, wait a minute, three times, we've already — you've already asked me to stay, or talked about me staying.

COMEY: And my common sense — again, I could be wrong, but my common sense told me what's going on here is that he's looking to get something in exchange for granting my request to stay in the job.

WARNER: And again, we all understand — I was a governor, I had people work for me. But this constant request — and, again, quoting you, him saying that he — despite you explaining your independence, he kept coming back to "I need loyalty." "I expect loyalty."

Had you ever had any of those kind of requests before, from anyone else you'd worked for in the government?

COMEY: No, and what made me uneasy was I'm, at that point, the director of the FBI. The reason that Congress created a ten-year term is so that the director is not feeling as if they're serving at — with political loyalty owed to any particular person.

The — the statue of Justice has a blindfold on because you're not supposed to be peeking out to see whether your patron is pleased or not with what you're doing.

It should be about the facts and the law. That's why I was — that's why I became FBI director: to be in that kind of position. So that's why I was so uneasy.

WARNER: Well, let me — let me move on. My time's running out. February 14th — again, it seems a bit strange. You were in a meeting. And your direct superior, the attorney general, was in that meeting, as well.

Yet the president asked everyone to leave, including the attorney general — to leave, before he brought up the matter of General Flynn. What was your impression of that type of action? Had you ever seen anything like that before?

COMEY: No. My impression was, something big is about to happen. I need to remember every single word that is spoken. And, again, I could be wrong, but I'm 56 years old. I've been — seen a few things.

My sense was the attorney general knew he shouldn't be leaving, which is why he was lingering. And I don't know Mr. Kushner well, but I think he picked up on the same thing. And so I knew something was about to happen that I needed to pay very close attention to.

WARNER: And I — I found it very interesting that, in the memo that you wrote after this February 14th pull-aside, you made clear that you wrote that memo in a way that was unclassified.

If you affirmatively made the decision to write a memo that was unclassified, was that because you felt, at some point, the facts of that meeting would have to come clean and come clear and actually be able to be cleared in a way that could be shared with the American people?

COMEY: Well, I remember thinking, this is a very disturbing development, really important to our work. I need to document it and preserve it in a way — and — and this committee gets this, but sometimes when things are classified, it tangles them up. It's hard...

WARNER: Amen.

COMEY:... to share it within an investigative team. It's — you have to be very careful about how you handle it, for good reason.

So my thinking was, if I write it in such a way that I don't include anything that would trigger a classification, that'll make it easier for us to discuss, within the FBI and the government, and to — to hold on to it in a way that makes it accessible to us.

WARNER: Well, again, it's our hope, particularly since you're a pretty knowledgeable guy and you wrote this in a way that was unclassified, that this committee will get access to that unclassified document. I think it'll be very important to our investigation.

Let me just ask this in closing: How many ongoing investigations, at any time, does the FBI have going on?

(CROSSTALK)

COMEY: Tens of thousands.

WARNER: Tens of thousands. Did the president ever ask about any other ongoing investigation?

COMEY: No.

WARNER: Did he ever ask about you trying to interfere on any other investigation?

COMEY: No.

WARNER: I think, again, this speaks volumes. This doesn't even get to the questions around the — the phone calls about lifting the cloud. I know other members will get to that, but I really appreciate your testimony and appreciate your service to our nation.

COMEY: Thank you, Senator Warner.

You know, I just — I'm sitting here, going through my contacts with him. I had one conversation with the president that was classified, where he asked about our — an ongoing intelligence investigation. It was brief and entirely professional.

WARNER: But he didn't ask you to take any specific action on that...

COMEY: No, no.

WARNER:... unlike what he had done vis-a-vis Mr. Flynn and the overall Russia investigation?

COMEY: Correct.

WARNER: Thank you, sir.

BURR: Senator Risch?

SENATOR JAMES RISCH: Thank you very much.

Mr. Comey, thank you for your service. America needs more like you, and we really appreciate it. Yesterday, I got, and everybody got, the seven pages of your direct testimony that's now a part of the record, here. And the first — I read it, then I read it again, and all I could think was, number one, how much I hated the class of legal writing when I was in law school.

And you were the guy that probably got the A, after — after reading this. So I — I find it clear, I find it concise and, having been a prosecutor for a number of years and handling hundred — maybe thousands of cases and read police reports, investigative reports, this is as good as it gets.

And — and I really appreciate that — not only — not only the conciseness and the clearness of it, but also the fact that you have things that were written down contemporaneously when they happened, and you actually put them in quotes, so we know exactly what happened and we're — and we're not getting some rendition of it that — that's in your mind. So...

COMEY: Thank you, Senator.

RISCH:... so you're — you're to be complimented for that.

COMEY: I had great parents and great teachers who beat that into me.

(CROSSTALK)

RISCH: That's obvious, sir.

The — the chairman walked you through a number of things that — that the American people need to know and want to know. Number one, obviously we're — all know about the active measures that the Russians have taken.

I think a lot of people were surprised at this. Those of us that work in the intelligence community didn't — it didn't come as a surprise. But now, the American people know this, and it's good they know this, because this is serious and it's a problem.

I — I think, secondly, I gather from all this that you're willing to say now that, while you were director, the president of the United States was not under investigation. Is that a fair statement?

COMEY: That's correct.

RISCH: All right. So that's a fact that we can rely at this...

COMEY: Yes, sir.

RISCH:... OK.

On — I remember, you — you talked with us shortly after February 14th, when the New York Times wrote an article that suggested that the Trump campaign was colluding with the Russians. You remember reading that article when it first came out?

COMEY: I do. It was about allegedly extensive electronic surveillance...

RISCH: Correct.

(CROSSTALK)

COMEY:... communications. Yes, sir.

RISCH: And — and that upset you to the point where you actually went out and surveyed the intelligence community to see whether — whether you were missing something in that. Is that correct?

COMEY: That's correct. I want to be careful in open setting. But...

RISCH: I — I'm — I'm not going to any further than that with it.

COMEY: OK.

RISCH: So thank you.

In addition to that, after that, you sought out both Republican and Democrat senators to tell them that, hey, I don't know where this is coming from, but this is not the — this is not factual. Do you recall that?

COMEY: Yes.

RISCH: OK. So — so, again, so the American people can understand this, that report by the New York Times was not true. Is that a fair statement?

COMEY: In — in the main, it was not true. And, again, all of you know this, maybe the American people don't. The challenge — and I'm not picking on reporters about writing stories about classified information, is that people talking about it often don't really know what's going on.

And those of us who actually know what's going on are not talking about it. And we don't call the press to say, hey, you got that thing wrong about this sensitive topic. We just have to leave it there.

I mentioned to the chairman the nonsense around what influenced me to make the July 5th statement. Nonsense, but I can't go explaining how it's nonsense.

RISCH: Thank you.

All right. So — so those three things, we now know, regarding the active measures, whether the president's under investigation and the collusion between the — the Russian — the Trump campaign and the

Russians.

I — I want to drill right down, as my time is limited, to the most recent dust-up regarding allegations that the president of the United States obstructed justice. And, boy, you nailed this down on page 5, paragraph 3. You put this in quotes — words matter.

You wrote down the words so we can all have the words in front of us now. There's 28 words there that are in quotes, and it says, quote, "I hope" — this is the president speaking — "I hope you can see your way clear to letting this go, to letting Flynn go. He is a good guy. I hope you can let this go."

Now those are his exact words, is that correct?

COMEY: Correct.

RISCH: And you wrote them here, and you put them in quotes?

COMEY: Correct.

RISCH: Thank you for that. He did not direct you to let it go.

COMEY: Not in his words, no.

RISCH: He did not order you to let it go.

COMEY: Again, those words are not an order.

RISCH: He said, "I hope." Now, like me, you probably did hundreds of cases, maybe thousands of cases charging people with criminal offenses. And, of course, you have knowledge of the thousands of cases out there that — where people have been charged.

Do you know of any case where a person has been charged for obstruction of justice or, for that matter, any other criminal offense, where this — they said, or thought, they hoped for an outcome?

COMEY: I don't know well enough to answer. And the reason I keep saying his words is I took it as a direction.

RISCH: Right.

COMEY: I mean, this is the president of the United States, with me alone, saying, "I hope" this. I took it as, this is what he wants me to do.

(CROSSTALK)

COMEY: Now I — I didn't obey that, but that's the way I took it.

RISCH: You — you may have taken it as a direction, but that's not what he said.

(CROSSTALK)

COMEY: Correct. I — that's why...

RISCH: He said — he said, "I hope."

COMEY: Those are exact words, correct.

RISCH: OK, do you — you don't know of anyone that's ever been charged for hoping something. Is that a fair statement?

COMEY: I don't, as I sit here.

RISCH: Yeah. Thank you.

Thank you, Mr. Chairman.

BURR: Senator Feinstein?

SENATOR DIANNE FEINSTEIN: Thanks very much, Mr. Chairman.

Mr. Comey, I just want you to know that I have great respect for you. Senator Cornyn and I sit on the Judiciary Committee, so we have occasion to have you before us. And I know that you're a man of strength and integrity, and I really regret the situation that we all find ourselves in. I just want to say that.

Let me begin with one overarching question. Why do you believe you were fired?

COMEY: Guess I don't know for sure. I believe the — I take the president at his word, that I was fired because of the Russia investigation.

Something about the way I was conducting it, the president felt, created pressure on him that he wanted to relieve.

Again, I didn't know that at the time, but I watched his interview, I've read the press accounts of his conversations. So I take him at his word there.

Now, look, I — I could be wrong. Maybe he's saying something that's not true. But I take him at his word, at least based on what I know now.

FEINSTEIN: Talk for a moment about his request that you pledge loyalty, and your response to that and what impact you believe that had.

COMEY: I — I don't know for sure, because I don't know the president well enough to read him well. I think it was — because our relationship didn't get off to a great start, given the conversation I had to have on January 6th, this was not — this didn't improve the relationship, because it was very, very awkward.

He was asking for something, and I was refusing to give it. But again, I don't know him well enough to know how he reacted to that, exactly.

FEINSTEIN: Do you believe the Russia investigation played a role?

COMEY: In why I was fired?

FEINSTEIN: Yes.

COMEY: Yes, because I've seen the president say so.

FEINSTEIN: OK. Let's — let's go to the Flynn issue.

Senator Risch outlined a — "I hope you could see your way (sic) to letting Flynn go. He's a good guy. I hope you can let this go."

But you also said, in your written remarks, and I quote, that you had "understood the president to be requesting that we drop any investigation of Flynn in connection with false statements about his conversations with the Russian ambassador in December," end quote. Please go into that with more detail.

COMEY: Well, the — the context and the president's words are what led me to that conclusion.

As I said in my statement, I could be wrong, but Flynn had been forced to resign the day before, and — and the controversy around General Flynn at that point in time was centered on whether he had lied to the vice president about the nature of his conversations with the Russians, whether he had been candid with others in the course of that.

And so that happens on the day before. On the 14th, the president makes specific reference to that. And so that's why I understood him to be saying that what he wanted me to do was drop any investigation connected to Flynn's account of his conversations with the Russians.

FEINSTEIN: Now, here's the question: You're big. You're strong. I know the Oval Office, and I know what happens to people when they walk in. There is a certain amount of intimidation. But why didn't you stop and say, "Mr. President, this is wrong. I cannot discuss this with you"?

COMEY: It's a great question. Maybe if I were stronger, I would have. I was so stunned by the conversation that I just...

(CROSSTALK)

COMEY:... took it in. And the only thing I could think to say, because I was playing in my mind, because I could remember every word he said — I was playing in my mind, what should my response be? And that's why I very carefully chose the words.

And, look, I — I've seen the tweet about tapes. Lordy, I hope there are tapes. I — I remember saying, "I agree he's a good guy," as a way of saying, "I'm not agreeing with what you just asked me to do."

Again, maybe other people would be stronger in that circumstance but that — that was — that's how I conducted myself. I — I hope I'll never have another opportunity. Maybe if I did it again, I would do it better.

FEINSTEIN: You described two phone calls that you received from President Trump, one on March 30 and one on April 11, where he, quote, "described the Russia investigation as a cloud that was impairing his ability," end quote, as president, and asked you, quote, "to lift the cloud," end quote.

What — how did you interpret that? And what did you believe he wanted you to do?

COMEY: I interpreted that as he was frustrated that the Russia investigation was taking up so much time and energy, I — I think he meant, of the executive branch, but in the — in the public square in general, and it was making it difficult for him to focus on other priorities of his. But what he asked me was actually narrower than that. So I think what he meant by the cloud, and again, I could be wrong, but what I think he meant by the cloud was the entire investigation is — is taking up oxygen and making it hard for me to focus on the things I want to focus on.

The ask was to get it out that I, the president, am not personally under investigation.

FEINSTEIN: After April 11th, did he ask you more, ever, about the Russia investigation? Did he ask you any questions?

COMEY: We never spoke again after April 11th.

FEINSTEIN: You told the president, I — I would see what we could do. What did you mean?

COMEY: Well, it was kind of a slightly cowardly way of trying to avoid telling him, we're not going to do that — that I would see what we could do. It was a way of kind of getting off the phone, frankly. And then I turned and handed it to the acting deputy attorney general, Mr. Boente.

FEINSTEIN: So I wanted to go into that. Who did you talk with about that — lifting the cloud, stopping the investigation — back at the FBI, and what was their response?

COMEY: Well, the FBI, during one of the two conversations — I'm not remembering exactly. I think the first — my chief of staff was actually sitting in front of me, and heard my end of the conversation, because the president's call was a surprise.

And I discussed the lifting the cloud and the request with the senior leadership team, who in — in — typically, and I think in all these circumstances, was the deputy director, my chief of staff, the general counsel, the deputy director's chief counsel and, I think, in a number of circumstances, the number three in the FBI, and a few of the conversations included the head of the national security branch, so that group of us that lead the FBI when it comes to national security.

FEINSTEIN: OK. You have the president of the United States asking you to stop an investigation that's an important investigation. What was the response of your colleagues?

COMEY: I think they were as shocked and troubled by it as I was. Some said things that led me to believe that. I don't remember exactly, but the reaction was similar to mine. They're all experienced people who had never experienced such a thing. So they were very concerned.

And then the conversation turned to about, so what should we do with this information? And that was a struggle for us, because we are the leaders of the FBI. So it's been reported to us, in that I heard it and now I've shared it with the leaders of the FBI — our — our conversation was, should we share this with any senior officials at the Justice Department?

Our — our absolute primary concern was, we can't infect the investigative team. We don't want the agents and analysts working on this to know the president of the United States has — has asked — and when it comes from the president, I took it as a direction — to get rid of this investigation, because we're not going to follow that — that request.

And so we decided we gotta keep it away from our troops. But is there anybody else we ought to tell at the Justice Department? And, as I laid out in my — in my statement, we considered whether to tell the attorney general, decided that didn't make sense because we believed, rightly, that he was shortly going to recuse.

There were no other Senate-confirmed leaders in the Justice Department at that point. The deputy attorney general was Mr. Boente, who was acting and going to be shortly in that seat. And we decided the best move would be to hold it, keep it in a box, document it as we'd already done, and then this investigation's going to go on — figure out what to do with it down the road.

Is there way to corroborate this? Our view, at the time, was, look, it's your word against the president's. There's no way to corroborate this. That — my view of that changed when the prospect of tapes was raised, but that's how we thought about it then.

FEINSTEIN: Thank you. Thank you, Mr. Chairman.

BURR: Senator Rubio.

SENATOR MARCO RUBIO: Thank you.

Director Comey, the meeting in the Oval Office where he made the request about Mike Flynn — was that the only time he asked you to hopefully let it go?

COMEY: Yes.

RUBIO: And in that meeting, as you understood it, that was — he was asking not about the general Russia investigation, he was asking very specifically about the jeopardy that Flynn was in himself?

COMEY: That's how I understood it, yes, sir.

RUBIO: And as you perceived it, while it was a request that — he hoped you did away with it, you perceived it as an order, given his position, the setting and the like, and some of the circumstances?

COMEY: Yes.

RUBIO: At the time, did you say anything to the president about — that is not an appropriate request, or did you tell the White House counsel, that is not an appropriate request, someone needs to go tell the president that he can't do these things?

COMEY: I didn't, no.

RUBIO: OK. Why?

COMEY: I don't know. I think the — as I said earlier, I think the circumstances were such that it was — I was a bit stunned, and didn't have the presence of mind.

And I don't know — you know, I don't want to make you — sound like I'm Captain Courageous. I don't know whether, even if I had the presence of mind, I would have said to the president, "Sir, that's wrong." I don't know whether I would have.

RUBIO: OK.

COMEY: But in the moment, it — it didn't — it didn't come to my mind. What came to my mind is, be careful what you say. And so I said, "I agree Flynn is a good guy."

RUBIO: So, on the cloud — we keep talking about this cloud — you perceived the cloud to be the Russian investigation in general, correct?

COMEY: Yes, sir.

RUBIO: But the specific ask was that you would tell the American people what you had already told him, what you had already told the leaders of Congress, both Democrats and Republicans: that he was not personally under investigation.

COMEY: Yes, sir, that's how I...

RUBIO: In fact, he was asking you to do what you have done here today.

COMEY:... correct. Yes, sir.

RUBIO: OK. And again, at that setting, did you say to the president that it would be inappropriate for you to do so, and then talk to the White House counsel or anybody so hopefully they would talk to him and tell him that he couldn't do this?

COMEY: First time, I said, "I'll see what we can do." Second time, I explained how it should work, that the White House counsel should contact the deputy attorney general.

RUBIO: You told him that?

COMEY: The president said, OK, then I think that's what I'll do.

RUBIO: And just to be clear, for you to make a public statement that he was not under investigation would not have been illegal, but you felt it made no sense because it could potentially create a duty to correct, if circumstances changed?

COMEY: Yes, sir. We wrestled with it before my testimony where I confirmed that there was an investigation. And there were two primary concerns. One was it creates a duty to correct, which I've lived before, and you want to be very careful about doing that.

And second, it's a slippery slope, because if we say the president and the vice president aren't under investigation, what's the principled basis for — for stopping?

RUBIO: OK.

COMEY: And so the leadership at — at justice, Acting Attorney General Boente, said, "You're not going to do that."

RUBIO: Now, on March 30th, during the phone call about General Flynn, you said he abruptly shifted and brought up something that you call, quote, unquote, "the McCabe thing." Specifically, the McCabe thing, as you understood it, was that McCabe's wife had received campaign money from what I assume means Terry McAuliffe...

COMEY: Yes, sir.

(CROSSTALK)

RUBIO:... who was very close to the Clintons. And — and so why did you — had the president at any point in time expressed to you concern, opposition, potential opposition to McCabe? "I don't like this guy because he got money from someone this close to Clinton?"

COMEY: He had asked me, during previous conversations, about Andy McCabe, and said, in essence, "How's he going to be with me as president? I was pretty rough on them on the campaign trail." And...

RUBIO: He was rough on McCabe?

COMEY:... he was — by his own account, he said he was rough on McCabe and Mrs. McCabe on the campaign trail — how's he going to be? And I assured the president, Andy is a total pro. No issue at all. You got to know the people of the FBI, they are not...

(CROSSTALK)

RUBIO: So — so, when the president turns to you and says, "Remember, I never brought up the McCabe thing because you said he was a good guy," did you perceive that to be a statement that — I took care of you, I — I didn't do something because you told me he was a good guy. So now, you know, I'm asking you, potentially, for something in return? Is that how you perceived it?

COMEY: I wasn't sure what to make of it, honestly. That's possible, but it — it was so out of context that I didn't have a clear view of what it was.

RUBIO: Now, on a number of occasions here, you bring up — let's talk now about the general Russia investigation, OK? In page 6 of your testimony, you say — the first thing you say is, he asked what we could do to, quote/unquote, "lift the cloud," the general Russia investigation.

And you responded that we were investigating the matter as quickly as we could and that there would be great benefit, if we didn't find anything, to having done the work well. And he agreed. He reemphasized the problems it was causing him, but he agreed.

So, in essence, the president agreed with your statement that it would be great if we could have an investigation, all the facts came out and we found nothing. So he agreed that that would be ideal, but this cloud is still messing up my ability to do the rest of my agenda. Is that an accurate assessment of...

(CROSSTALK)

COMEY: Yes, sir. He actually went farther than that. He — he said, "And if some of my satellites did something wrong, it'd be good to find that out."

RUBIO: Well, that's the second part, and that is the satellites. He said, "If one of my satellites" — I imagine, by that, he meant some of the other people surrounding his campaign — "did something wrong, it would be great to know that, as well"?

COMEY: Yes, sir. That's what he said.

RUBIO: So are those the other — are those the only two instances in which that sort of back-and-forth happened, where the president was basically saying, and I'm paraphrasing here, it's OK, do the Russia investigation. I hope it all comes out. I have nothing to do with anything Russia. It'd be great if it all came out, if people around me were doing things that were wrong.

COMEY: Yes. As I — I recorded it accurately there. That was the sentiment he was expressing. Yes, sir.

RUBIO: So what it basically comes down to is the president has asked three things of you. He asked for your loyalty, and you said you would be loyally honest.

COMEY: Honestly loyal.

RUBIO: Honestly loyal. The — the — he asked you, on one occasion, to let the Mike Flynn thing go because he was a good guy — but you're aware that he said the exact same thing in the press the next day. "He's a good guy," "He's been treated unfairly," et cetera, et cetera. So I imagine your FBI agents read that.

(CROSSTALK)

COMEY: I'm sure they did.

RUBIO: Your — the president's wishes were known to them, certainly, by the next day, when he had a press conference with the prime minister. But going back, the three requests were; number one, be loyal; number two, let the Mike Flynn thing go, he's a good guy, he's been treated unfairly; and, number three, can you please tell the American people what these leaders in Congress already know, what you already know, what you've told me three times — that I'm not under — personally under investigation?

COMEY: Those are the three things he asked. Yes, sir.

RUBIO: You know, this investigation is full of leaks, left and right. I mean, we've learned more from the newspapers sometimes than we do from our open hearings, for sure.

You ever wonder why, of all the things in this investigation, the only thing that's never been leaked is the fact that the president was not personally under investigation, despite the fact that both Democrats and Republicans in the leadership of Congress knew that, and have known that for weeks?

COMEY: I don't know. I find matters that are briefed to the Gang of Eight are pretty tightly held, in my experience.

RUBIO: Finally, who are those senior leaders at the FBI that you shared these conversations with?

COMEY: As I said in response to Senator Feinstein's question, deputy director, my chief of staff, general counsel, the deputy director's chief counsel, and then, more often than not, the number three person at the FBI, who is the associate deputy director, and then, quite often, the head of the national security branch.

BURR: Senator Wyden.

SENATOR RON WYDEN: Thank you, Mr. Chairman.

Mr. Comey, welcome. You and I have had significant policy differences over the years, particularly protecting Americans' access to secure encryption. But I believe the timing of your firing stinks.

And yesterday, you put on the record testimony that demonstrates why the odor of presidential abuse of power is so strong.

Now, to my questions. In talking to Senator Warner about this dinner that you had with president, I believe, January 27th, all in one dinner, the president raised your job prospects, he asked for your loyalty and denied allegations against him — all took place over one supper. Now, you told Senator Warner that the president was looking to, quote, "get something." Looking back, did that dinner suggest that your job might be contingent on how you handled the investigation?

COMEY: I don't know that I'd go that far. I — I got the sense my job would be contingent upon how he felt I — excuse me — how he felt I conducted myself and whether I demonstrated loyalty. But I don't know whether I'd go so far as to connect it to the investigation.

(CROSSTALK)

WYDEN: You said the president was trying to create some sort of patronage relationship. In a patronage relationship isn't the underling expected to behave in a manner consistent with the wishes of the boss?

COMEY: Yes.

WYDEN: OK.

COMEY: Or at least consider how what you're doing will affect the boss as a significant consideration.

WYDEN: Let me turn to the Attorney General. In your statement, you said that you and the FBI leadership team decided not to discuss the president's actions with Attorney General Sessions, even though he had not recused himself.

What was it about the Attorney General's own interactions with the Russians, or his behavior with regard to the investigation, that would have led the entire leadership of the FBI to make this decision?

COMEY: Our judgment, as I recall, was that he was very close to and inevitably going to recuse himself for a variety of reasons. We also were aware of facts that I can't discuss in an open setting that would make his continued engagement in a Russia-related investigation problematic.

And so we were — we were convinced — and, in fact, I think we had already heard that the career people were recommending that he recuse himself — that he was not going to be in contact with Russia-related matters much longer, and that turned out to be the case.

WYDEN: How would you characterize Attorney General Sessions's adherence to his recusal, in particular with regard to his involvement in your firing, which the president has acknowledged was because of the Russian investigation?

COMEY: That's a question I can't answer. I think it's a reasonable question. If — if, as the president said, I was fired because of the Russia investigation, why was the attorney general involved in that chain? I don't know, and so I don't have an answer for the question.

WYDEN: Your testimony was that the president's request about Flynn could infect the investigation. Had the president got what he wanted and what he asked of you, what would have been the effect on the investigation?

COMEY: Well we would have closed any investigation of General

Flynn in connection with his statements and encounter — statements about and encounters with Russians in the late part of December.

WYDEN: Well...

(CROSSTALK)

COMEY: So we — we would have dropped an open criminal investigation.

WYDEN: So, in effect, when you talk about infecting the enterprise, you would have dropped something major that would have spoken to the overall ability of the American people to get the facts?

COMEY: Correct. And — and, as good as our people are, our judgment was we don't want them hearing that the president of the United States wants this to go away, because it might have an effect of their ability to be fair and impartial and aggressive.

WYDEN: Now, the — Acting Attorney General Yates found out that Michael Flynn could be blackmailed by the Russians, and she went immediately to warn the White House.

Flynn is gone, but other individuals with contacts with the Russians are still in extremely important positions of power. Should the American people have the same sense of urgency now, with respect to them?

COMEY: I think all I can say, Senator, is it's a — the special counsel's investigation is very important. Understanding what efforts there were or are by the Russian government to influence our government is a critical part of the FBI's mission, so — and you've got the right person in Bob Mueller to lead it.

So it's a very important piece of work.

WYDEN: Vice President Pence was the head of the transition. To your knowledge, was he aware of the concerns about Michael Flynn prior to or during General Flynn's tenure as national security adviser?

COMEY: I don't — you're asking — including up to the time when Flynn was...

WYDEN: Right.

COMEY:... forced to resign? My understanding is that he was, and I'm trying to remember where I get that understanding from — I think from Acting Attorney General Yates.

WYDEN: So former Acting Attorney General Yates testified that concerns about General Flynn were discussed with the intelligence community. Would that have included anyone at the CIA or Dan Coats' office at the DNI?

COMEY: I would assume yes.

WYDEN: Michael Flynn resigned four days after Attorney General Sessions was sworn in. Do you know if the attorney general was aware of the concerns about Michael Flynn during that period?

COMEY: I don't, as I sit here — I don't — I don't recall that he was. I could be wrong, but I don't remember that he was.

WYDEN: And, finally, let's see if you can give us some sense of who recommended your firing. Besides the letters from the attorney general, the deputy attorney general, do you have any information on who may have recommended or have been involved in your firing?

COMEY: I don't. I don't.

WYDEN: OK.

Thank you, Mr. Chairman.

BURR: Senator Collins.

SENATOR SUSAN COLLINS: Thank you, Mr. Chairman.

Mr. Comey, let me begin by thanking you for your voluntary compliance with our request to appear before this committee, and it's discussing this very important investigation.

I want, first, to ask you about your conversations with the president, the three conversations in which you told him that he was not under investigation.

The first was during your January 6th meeting, according to your testimony, in which it appears that you actually volunteered that assurance. Is that correct?

COMEY: That's correct.

COLLINS: Did you limit that statement to counterintelligence investigations, or were you talking about any kind of FBI investigation?

COMEY: I didn't — I didn't use the term "counterintelligence." I was speaking to him, and briefing him about some salacious and unverified material. It was in the context of that that he had a strong and defensive reaction about that not being true. And my reading of it was it was important for me to assure him we were not personally investigating him. And so the context then was actually narrower, focused on what I had just talked to him about.

It was very important because it was, first, true. And second, I was worried very much about being in kind of a — kind of a J. Edgar Hoover-type situation. I didn't want him thinking that I was briefing him on this to sort of hang it over him in some way. I was briefing him on it because we were — had been told by the media it was about to launch. We didn't want to be keeping that from him.

COMEY: And if there was some — he needed to know this was being said. But I was very keen not to leave him with an impression that the bureau was trying to do something to him. And so that's the context in which I said, "Sir, we're not personally investigating you."

COLLINS: And then, on — and that's why you volunteered the information...

COMEY: Yes, ma'am.

COLLINS:... correct?

Then, on the January 27th dinner, you show — you told the president that he should be careful about asking you to investigate, because, quote, "You might create a narrative that we are investigating him personally," which we weren't.

Again, were you limiting that statement to counterintelligence investigations, or more broadly, such as a criminal investigation?

COMEY: The context was very similar. I didn't — I didn't modify the word "investigation." It was — again, he was reacting strongly again to that unverified material, saying, "I'm tempted to order you to investigate it." And that — in the context of that, I said "Sir, you want to be careful about that, because it might create a narrative we're investigating you personally."

COLLINS: And then there was the March 30th phone call in — with the president, in which you reminded him that congressional leaders have been briefed that we were not personally — the FBI was not personally investigating President Trump.

And again, was that statement to congressional leaders and to the president limited to counterintelligence investigations? Or was it a broader statement?

(CROSSTALK)

COLLINS: I'm trying to understand whether there was any kind of investigation of the president under way.

COMEY: No. I'm sorry, and — and if I misunderstood, I apologize. We briefed the congressional leadership about what Americans we had opened counterintelligence investigation cases on, and we specifically said the president is not one of those Americans, but — that there was no other investigation of the president that we were not mentioning at that time.

What — the context was counterintelligence, but I wasn't trying to hide some criminal investigation of the president.

COLLINS: And was the president under investigation at the time of your dismissal on May 9th?

COMEY: No.

COLLINS: I'd like to now turn to the conversations with the president about Michael Flynn, which have been discussed at great length. And, first, let me make very clear that the president never should have cleared the room, and he never should have asked you, as you reported, to let it go — to let the investigation go.

But I remain puzzled by your response. Your response was, "I agree that Michael Flynn is a good guy." You could have said, "Mr. President, this meeting is inappropriate. This response could compromise the investigation. You should not be making such a request."

It's fundamental to the operation of our government that the FBI be insulated from this kind of political pressure. And you've talked a bit today about that you were stunned by the president making the request.

But my question to you is, later on, upon reflection, did you go to anyone at the Department of Justice and ask them to call the White House counsel's office and explain that the president had to have a far better understanding and appreciation of his role vis-a-vis the FBI?

COMEY: In general, I did. I spoke to the attorney general, and I spoke to the new deputy attorney general, Mr. Rosenstein, when he took office, and explained my serious concern about the way in which the president is interacting, especially with the FBI.

And I specifically, as I said my testimony, asked the — told the attorney general, it can't happen that you get kicked out of the room and the president talks to me.

Look, in the room — and — and — but why didn't we raise the specific? It was of investigative interest us to try and figure out, so — what just happened with the president's request. So I would not have wanted to alert the White House that it had happened until we figured out, what are we going to do with this investigatively?

COLLINS: Your testimony was that you went to Attorney General Sessions and said, "Don't ever leave me alone with him again." Are you saying that you also told him that he had made a request that you let it go, with regard to part of the investigation of Michael Flynn?

COMEY: No, I specifically did not. I did not.

COLLINS: OK, you mentioned that, from your very first meeting with the president, you decided to write a memo memorializing the conversation. What was it about that very first meeting that made you write a memo, when you had not done that with two previous presidents?

COMEY: As I said, a combination of things. A gut feeling is an important overlay on it. But the circumstances — that I was alone, the subject matter, and the nature of the person that I was interacting with and my read of that person.

(UNKNOWN): The nature of that person?

COMEY: Yeah, and — and — and, really, just a gut feel, laying on top of all of that, that this — it's going to be important, to protect this organization, that I make records of this.

COLLINS: And finally, did you show copies of your memos to anyone outside of the Department of Justice?

COMEY: Yes.

COLLINS: And to whom did you show copies?

COMEY: I asked — the president tweeted on Friday, after I got fired, that I better hope there's not tapes. I woke up in the middle of the night on Monday night, because it didn't dawn on me originally that there might be corroboration for our conversation. There might be a tape.

And my judgment was, I needed to get that out into the public square. And so I asked a friend of mine to share the content of the memo with a reporter. Didn't do it myself, for a variety of reasons. But I asked him to, because I thought that might prompt the appointment of a special counsel. And so I asked a close friend of mine to do it.

COLLINS: And was that Mr. Wittes?

COMEY: No, no.

COLLINS: Who was that?

COMEY: A good friend of mine who's a professor at Columbia Law School.

COLLINS: Thank you.

BURR: Senator Heinrich?

SENATOR MARTIN HEINRICH: Mr. Comey, prior to January 27th of this year, have you ever had a one-on-one meeting or — or a private dinner with a president of the United States?

COMEY: No, I met — dinner, no. I had two one-on-ones with President Obama that I laid out in my testimony: once, to talk about law enforcement issues — law enforcement and race, which was an important topic throughout for me and for the president; and then once, very briefly, for him to say goodbye.

HEINRICH: Were those brief interactions?

COMEY: No. The one about law enforcement and race in policing, we spoke for probably over an hour, just the two of us.

HEINRICH: How unusual is it to have a — a one-on-one dinner with the president? Did that strike you as odd?

COMEY: Yeah, so much so that I assumed there would be others — that he couldn't possibly be having dinner with me alone.

HEINRICH: If — do you have an impression that, if you had found — if you had behaved differently in that dinner — and I am quite pleased that you did not — but if you had found a way to express some sort of expression of loyalty, or given some suggestion that the Flynn criminal investigation might be pursued less vigorously, do you think you would've still been fired?

COMEY: I don't know. I — it's impossible to say, looking back. I don't know.

HEINRICH: But you felt like those two things were — were directly relevant to your — the kind of relationship that the president was seeking to establish with you?

COMEY: Sure, yes.

HEINRICH: The — the president has repeatedly talked about the Russian investigation into the U.S. — or the Russian — Russia's involvement in the U.S. election cycle as a hoax and as fake news.

Can you talk a little bit about what you saw as FBI director — and, obviously, only the parts that you can share in this setting — that — that demonstrate how serious this action actually was, and why there was an investigation in the first place?

COMEY: Yes, sir. The — there should be no fuzz on this whatsoever. The Russians interfered in our election during the 2016 cycle. They did it with purpose. They did it with sophistication. They did it with overwhelming technical efforts. And it was an active-measures campaign driven from the top of that government. There is no fuzz on that.

It is a high-confidence judgment of the entire intelligence community, and — and the members of this committee have — have seen the intelligence. It's not a close call. That happened. That's about as unfake as you can possibly get, and is very, very serious, which is why it's so refreshing to see a bipartisan focus on that, because this is about America, not about any particular party.

HEINRICH: So that was a hostile act by the Russian government against this country?

COMEY: Yes, sir.

HEINRICH: Did the president, in any of those interactions that you've shared with us today, ask you what you should be doing, or what our government should be doing, or the intelligence community, to protect America against Russian interference in our election system?

COMEY: I don't recall a conversation like that.

HEINRICH: Never?

COMEY: No.

HEINRICH: Do you — do you find it odd...

(CROSSTALK)

COMEY: Not with — not with — not with President Trump.

HEINRICH: Right.

COMEY: I attended a fair number of meetings on that with President Obama.

HEINRICH: Do you find it odd that the president seemed unconcerned by Russia's actions in our election?

COMEY: I — I can't answer that, because I don't know what other conversations he had with other advisers or other intelligence community leaders. So I — I — I just don't know, sitting here.

HEINRICH: Did you have any interactions with the president that suggested he was taking that hostile action seriously?

COMEY: I don't remember any interactions with the president, other than the initial briefing on January the 6th. I don't remember — could be wrong, but I don't remember any conversations with him at all about that.

HEINRICH: As you're very aware, it was only the two of you in the room for that dinner. You've told us the president asked you to back off the Flynn investigation. The president told a reporter...

COMEY: Not in that dinner.

HEINRICH: Fair enough — told the reporter he did — never did that. You've testified that the president asked for your loyalty in that dinner. The White House denies that. A lot of this comes down to, who should we believe? Do you want to say anything as to why we should believe you?

COMEY: Probably — my mother raised me not to say things like this about myself, so not I'm going to. I think people should look at the whole body of my testimony, because, as I used to say to juries, and when I talked about a witness, you can't cherry-pick it. You can't say, "I like these things he said, but on this, he's a — he's a dirty, rotten liar."

HEINRICH: Right.

COMEY: You got to take it all together. And I've tried to be open and fair and transparent and accurate. A really significant fact to me is, so why did he kick everybody out of the Oval Office? Why would you kick the attorney general, the president, the chief of staff out, to talk to me, if it was about something else? And so that — that, to me, is — as an investigator, is a very significant fact.

HEINRICH: And as we look at — at testimony, or as — communication from both of you, we should probably be looking for consistency.

COMEY: Well, in looking at any witness, you look at consistency, track record, demeanor, record over time, that sort of thing.

HEINRICH: Thank you.

So there are reports that the incoming Trump administration, either during the transition and/or after the inauguration, attempted to set up a sort of back-door communication channel with the Russian government using their infrastructure, their devices or facilities.

What would be the risks particularly for a transition, someone not actually in the office of the president yet, to setting up unauthorized channels with a hostile foreign government, especially if they were to evade our own American intelligence services?

COMEY: I'm not going to comment on whether that happened in an open setting. But the risk is — primary risk is obvious: you spare the Russians the cost and effort of having to break into our communications channels by using theirs.

And so you make it a whole lot easier for them to capture all of your conversations, and then to use those to the benefit of Russia against the United States.

HEINRICH: The memos that you wrote — you wrote, did you write all nine of them in a way that was designed to prevent them from needing classification?

COMEY: No. And — and, on a few of the occasions, I wrote — I sent e-mails to my chief of staff or others on some of the brief phone conversations that I recall. The first one was a classified briefing.

Although it wasn't in a SCIF, it was in a conference room at Trump Tower. It was a classified briefing and so I wrote that on a classified device. The one I started typing...

HEINRICH: Got you.

COMEY:... in the car — that was a classified laptop that I started working on.

HEINRICH: Any reason, in a classified environment, in a SCIF, that this committee would — it would not be appropriate to see those communications, from — at least from your perspective as the author?

COMEY: No.

HEINRICH: Thank you, Mr. Chairman.

BURR: Senator Blunt.

SENATOR ROY BLUNT: Thank you, Mr. Chairman.

Mr. Comey, when you were terminated at the FBI, I said, and still continue to feel, that you have provided years of great service to the country.

I also said that I'd had significant questions, over the last year, about some of the decision you made. If — if the president hadn't terminated your service, would you still be, in your opinion, the director of the FBI today?

COMEY: Yes, sir.

BLUNT: So you took as a direction from the president something that you thought was serious and troublesome, but continued to show up for work the next day?

COMEY: Yes, sir.

BLUNT: And, six weeks later we're still telling the — we're telling the president, on March the 30th, that he was not personally the target of any investigation?

COMEY: Correct. On March the 30th, and I think again on — I think on April 11th as well, I told him we're not investigating him personally. That was true.

BLUNT: Well, the point to me — the concern to me there is that all these things are going on. You, now, in retrospect — or at you, now, to this committee — that these were — you had serious concerns about what the president had, you believed, directed you to do, and had taken no action — hadn't even reported up the chain of command, assuming you believe there is an "up the chain of command," that these things had happened.

Do you have a sense of that, looking back, that that was a mistake?

COMEY: No. In fact, I think no action was the most important thing I could do to make sure there was no interference with the investigation.

BLUNT: And on the — on the Flynn issue specifically, I believe you said earlier that you believed the president was suggesting you drop any investigation of Flynn's account of his conversation with the Russian ambassador, which was essentially misleading the vice president and others?

COMEY: Correct, and — and I'm not going to go into the details, but whether there were false statements made to government investigators, as well.

BLUNT: The — any suggestion that the — that General Flynn had violated the Logan Act, I always find pretty incredible. The Logan Act's been on the books for over 200 years. Nobody's ever been prosecuted for violating the Logan Act.

My sense would be that the discussion — not the problem — misleading investigators or the vice president might have been.

COMEY: That's fair. Yes, sir.

BLUNT: And — and you're — had you previously, on February the 14th, discussed with the president, in the previous meeting, anything your investigators had learned, or their impressions from talking to Flynn?

COMEY: No, sir.

BLUNT: So he said, "He's a good guy." You said, "He's a good guy." And that was — no further action taken on that?

COMEY: Well, he said more than that. But there was no — the action was I wrote it up, briefed our senior team, tried to figure out what to do with it and just made a decision, we're going to hold this and then see what we make of it down the road.

COMEY: Yes, sir.

BLUNT: Was it your view that not briefing up meant you really had no responsibility to report that to the Justice Department in some way?

COMEY: I think, at some point — and — and I don't know what Director Mueller is going to do with it, but at some point I was sure we were going to brief it to the team in charge of the case.

But our judgment was, in the short term, doesn't make sense to — no fuzz on the fact that I reported it to the attorney general. That's why I stressed he shouldn't be kicked out of the room. But — didn't make sense to report to him now.

BLUNT: You know, you said the attorney general said, "I don't want to be in the room with him alone again," but you continued to talk to him on the phone. What is the difference in being in the room alone with him and talking to him on the phone alone?

COMEY: Yeah, I think that what I stressed to the attorney general was a little broader than just the room. I said "You — I report to you. It's very important you be between me and the White House, between..."

(CROSSTALK)

BLUNT: After that discussion with the attorney general, did you take phone calls from the president?

COMEY: Yes, sir.

BLUNT: So why did you just say you need to talk to — why didn't you say, "I'm not taking that call. You need to talk to the attorney general"?

COMEY: Well, I — I did, on the April 11th call, and I reported the calls — the March 30th call and the April 11th call — to my superior, who was the acting deputy attorney general.

BLUNT: I — I don't want to run out of time here. Let me make one other point.

In reading your testimony, January the 3rd, January the 27th and March the 30th — it appears to me that, on all three of those occa-

sions, you, unsolicited by the president, made the point to him that
he was not a target of the — of an investigation.

COMEY: Correct. Yes, sir.

BLUNT: One, I thought the March 30th very interesting. You said,
well, even though you don't want — you may not want us — that
was the 27th, where he said, "Why don't you look into that dossier
thing more?" You said, "Well, you may not want that, because then we
couldn't tell you — couldn't say with — we couldn't answer the question about you being a target of the investigation."

But you didn't seem to be answering that question anyhow. As Senator Rubio pointed out, the one unanswered, unleaked question seems
to have been that, in this whole period of time.

But you said something earlier I don't want to fail to follow up on. You
said, after you were dismissed, you gave information to a friend so
that friend could get that information into the public media.

COMEY: Correct.

BLUNT: What kind of information was that? Wasn't that — what
kind of information did you give to a friend?

COMEY: That the — the — the Flynn conversation, that the president asked me to let the — the Flynn — I'm forgetting my exact own
words, but the — the conversation in the Oval Office.

BLUNT: So you didn't consider your memo or your sense of that
conversation to be a government document? You consider it to be
somehow your own personal document that you could share with the
media as you wanted to?

COMEY: Correct. I...

BLUNT: Through a friend?

COMEY:... I understood this to be my recollection, recorded, of my
conversation with the president. As a private citizen, I felt free to
share that. I thought it very important to get it out.

BLUNT: So were all of your memos that you've recorded on classified or other documents memos that might be yours as a private citizen?

COMEY: I'm sorry, I'm not following the question.

BLUNT: Well, I think you said you'd used classified — a classified...

(CROSSTALK)

COMEY: Not the classified documents. Unclassified — I don't have any of them anymore. I gave them to the special counsel. But, yeah, my view was that the content of those unclassified — the memorialization of those conversations was my recollection recorded.

BLUNT: So why didn't you give those to somebody yourself, rather than give them through a third party?

COMEY: Because I was worried the media was camping at the end of my driveway at that point, and I was actually going out of town with my wife to hide, and I worried it would be like feeding seagulls at the beach...

(LAUGHTER)

...if — if it was — if it was I who gave it to the media. So I asked my friend, "Make sure this gets out."

BLUNT: It does seem to me that what you do there is create a source close to the former director of the FBI, as opposed to just taking responsibility yourself for saying, "Here are these records."

And, like everybody else, I have other things I'd like to get into, but I'm out of time.

COMEY: OK.

BURR: Senator King.

SENATOR ANGUS KING: Thank you.

First I'd like to acknowledge Senator Blumenthal and, earlier, Senator Nelson. I think the one principal thing you'll learn today, Senator, is that the chairs there are less comfortable than the chairs here. But I welcome you to the hearing.

Mr. Comey, a broad question. Was the Russian activity in the 2016 election a one-off proposition? Or is this part of a long-term strategy? Will they be back?

COMEY: Oh, it's a long-term practice of theirs. It — it stepped up a notch in a significant way in '16. They'll be back.

KING: I think that's very important for the American people to understand, that this is — this is very much a forward-looking investigation in terms of how do we understand what they did and how do we prevent it. Would you agree that that's a big part of our role here?

COMEY: Yes, sir, and it's not a Republican thing or Democratic thing. It really is an American thing. They're going to come for whatever party they choose to try and work on behalf of. And they're — they're not devoted to either, in my experience. They're just about their own advantage. And they will be back.

KING: That's my observation. I don't think Putin is a Republican or a Democrat. He's an opportunist.

COMEY: I think that's a fair statement.

KING: With regard to the — several of these conversations, in his interview with Lester Holt on NBC, the president said, "I had dinner with him. He wanted to have dinner because he wanted to stay on." Is this an accurate statement?

COMEY: No, sir.

KING: Did you, in any way, initiate that dinner?

COMEY: No, he — he called me at my desk at lunchtime, and asked me was I free for dinner that night. I called himself and said, "Can you come over for dinner tonight?"

And I said, "Yes, sir."

He said, "Will 6 work?" I think he said 6 first. And then he said, "I was going to invite your whole family, but we'll do that next time. I wanted you to come over. And is — is that a good time?"

I said, "Sir, whatever works for you."

And he then said, "How about 6:30?"

And I — I said, "Whatever works for you, sir." And then I hung up and had to call my wife and break a date with her. I was supposed to take her out to dinner that night, and (OFF-MIKE).

KING: That's one of the all-time great excuses for breaking a date.

(LAUGHTER)

COMEY: In retrospect, I would have — I love spending time my wife. I wish I'd been there that night. (LAUGHTER)

KING: That's one question I'm not going follow up, Mr. Comey.

But, in that same interview, the president said, "In one case, I called him, and in one case, he called me." Is that an accurate statement?

COMEY: No.

KING: Did you ever call the president?

COMEY: No. I — I might — the only reason I'm hesitating is I think there was a least one conversation where I was asked to call the White House switchboard to be connected to him, but I — I never initiated a communication with the president.

KING: And, in his press conference on May 18th, the president was asked whether he had urged you to shut down the investigation into Michael Flynn. The president responded, quote, "No, no. Next question." Is that an accurate statement?

COMEY: I don't believe it is.

KING: Thank you.

With regard to the question of him being under personal — personally under investigation, does that mean that the dossier is not being reviewed or investigated or followed up on in any way?

COMEY: I obviously can't — I can't comment either way. I can't talk in an open setting about the investigation as it was when I was the head of the FBI. And obviously it's — it's Director Mueller's — Bob Mueller's responsibility now, so I just — I don't know.

KING: So clearly your statements to the president back in those — these various times when you assured him he wasn't under investigation were as of that moment. That — that correct, is it not?

COMEY: Correct — correct.

KING: Now, on the Flynn investigation, is it not true that Mr. Flynn was and is a central figure in this entire investigation of the relationship between the Trump campaign and the Russians?

COMEY: I can't answer that in an open setting, sir.

KING: And certainly Mr. Flynn was part of the so-called Russian investigation. Can you answer that question?

COMEY: I have to give you the same answer.

KING: All right. We'll be having a closed session shortly, so we will follow up on that.

In terms of his comments to you about — I think in response to Mr. Risch — to Senator Risch, you said he said, "I hope you will hold back on that." But when you get a — when a president of the United States in the Oval Office says something like "I hope" or "I suggest" or — or "would you," do you take that as a — as a — as a directive?

COMEY: Yes. Yes, it rings in my ear as kind of, "Will no one rid me of this meddlesome priest?"

KING: I was just going to quote that. In 1170, December 29, Henry II said, "Who will rid me of this meddlesome priest?" and then, the next day, he was killed — Thomas Becket. That's exactly the same situation. You're — we're thinking along the same lines.

Several other questions, and these are a little bit more detailed. What do you know about the Russian bank, VEB?

COMEY: Nothing that I can talk about in an open setting. I mean, I know it...

(CROSSTALK)

KING: Well, that takes care of my next three questions.

COMEY: I know it exists. Yes, sir.

KING: You know it exists. What is the relationship of Ambassador — the ambassador from Russia to the United States, to the Russian intelligence infrastructure?

COMEY: Well, he's a diplomat who is the chief of mission at the Russian embassy, which employs a robust cohort of intelligence officers. And so, surely, he's witting of their very, very aggressive intelligence operations, at least some of it in the United States. I don't — I don't consider him to be an intelligence officer himself. He's a diplomat.

KING: Did you ever — did the FBI ever brief the Trump administration about the — the advisability of interacting directly with Ambassador Kislyak?

COMEY: Look, all I can say sitting here is there were a variety of defensive briefings given to the incoming administration about the counterintelligence risk.

KING: Back to Mr. Flynn, would the — would closing out the Flynn investigation have impeded the overall Russian investigation?

COMEY: No. Well, unlikely, except to the extent — there's always a possibility, if you have a criminal case against someone and you bring in and squeeze them, you flip them, and they give you information about something else. But I saw the two as touching each other, but separate.

KING: With regard to your memos, isn't it true that in a — in a court case, when you're weighing evidence, contemporaneous memos and contemporaneous statements to third parties are considered probative in terms of the — the — the validity of — of testimony?

COMEY: Yes.

KING: Thank you.

Thank you, Mr. Chairman.

BURR: Senator Cotton?

Or — excuse me, Senator Lankford?

SENATOR JAMES LANKFORD: Well, Director Comey, good to see you again.

COMEY: You, too.

LANKFORD: We've had multiple opportunities to be able to visit, as everyone on this dais has. And I appreciate you and your service and what you have done for the nation for a long time, which you continue to do.

I've told you before in the heat of last year, when we had an opportunity to visit personally, that I pray for you and for your family, because you do carry a tremendous amount of stress. And that is still true today.

COMEY: Thank you.

LANKFORD: Let me — let me walk through a couple things with you. Your notes were obviously exceptionally important, because they give a very rapid account of what you — what you wrote down and what you perceived to happen in those different meetings.

Have you had the opportunity to be able to reference those notes when you were preparing the written statement that you put — for us today?

COMEY: Yes, I — yes. I think nearly all of my written recordings of my conversations — had a chance to review them before filing my statement.

LANKFORD: Do you have a copy of any those notes, personally?

COMEY: I don't. I turned them over to Bob Mueller's investigators.

LANKFORD: The individual that you told about your memos, that then sent on to the New York Times — do they have a copy of those memos, or were they told orally of those memos?

COMEY: Had a copy — had a copy at the time.

LANKFORD: Do they — do they still have a copy of those memos?

COMEY: That's a good question. I think so. I guess I can't say for sure, sitting here, but I — I — I guess I don't know, but I think so.

LANKFORD: So the question is, could you ask them to hand that copy right back to you, so you could hand them over to this committee?

COMEY: Potentially.

LANKFORD: I would like to move that from "potential" to "see if we can ask that question," so we can have a copy of those. Obviously those notes are exceptionally important to us to be able to go through the process so we can — we can continue to get to the facts as — as we see it. As you know, the written documents are exceptionally important. Are there other documents that we need to be aware of that you used in your preparation for your written statement that we should also have, that would assist us in helping with this?

COMEY: Not that I'm aware of, no.

LANKFORD: Past the February the 14th meeting which is a very important meeting obviously, as we discuss the conversations here about Michael Flynn. When the president asked you about he hopes that you would let this go, and the conversation back and forth about him being a good guy.

After that time did the president ever bring up anything about Michael Flynn again to you? You had multiple other conversations you have (inaudible) with the president.

COMEY: No, I don't remember him ever bringing it up again.

LANKFORD: Did any member of the White House staff ever come to you and talk to you about letting go of the Michael Flynn case, or dropping it or anything referring to that?

COMEY: No, nope.

LANKFORD: Did the director of national intelligence come to you and talk to you about that?

COMEY: No.

LANKFORD: Did anyone from the Attorney General's office, the Department of Justice ask you about that?

COMEY: No.

LANKFORD: Did the head of NSA talk to you about that?

COMEY: No.

LANKFORD: The — the key aspect here is, if — if — if this seems to be something the president's trying to get you to drop it, this seems like a pretty light touch to drop it, to bring it up at that moment the day after he had just fired Flynn to come back in and say I hope we can let this go.

But then it never reappears again. Did — did it slow down your investigation or any investigation that may or may not be occurring with Michael Flynn?

COMEY: No, although I don't know there're any manifestations — our manifestations of the investigation between February 14th and when I was fired. So I — I don't know that the president had any way of knowing whether it was effective or not.

LANKFORD: OK. That's fair enough. If — if the president wanted to stop an investigation, how would he do that? Knowing it's an ongoing criminal investigation or counterintelligence investigation.

Would that be a matter of trying to go to you — you perceive and to say you make it stop because he doesn't have the authority to stop or how — how would the president make an ongoing investigation stop?

COMEY: Again, I'm not a legal scholar. So smarter people answer this better, but I think as a legal matter, president is the head of the executive branch and could direct, in theory, we have important norms against this, but direct that anybody be investigated or anybody not be investigated.

I think he has the legal authority because all of us ultimately report in the executive branch up to the president.

LANKFORD: OK. Would that be to you, would that be the attorney general? Would that be to who that would do that?

COMEY: Suppose he could do it to — if he wanted to issue a direct order, could do it in any way, could do it through the attorney general or issue it directly to me.

LANKFORD: Well — well, is there any question that the president is not real fond of this investigation? I — I can think of multiple 140 word — character expressions that he's done publicly to express he's not fond of the investigation.

So I've heard you share before in this conversation that you're trying to keep the agents that are working on it away from any comment the president might have made. Quite frankly, the president has informed around 6 billion people that he's not real fond of this investigation.

Do you think there's a difference in that?

COMEY: Yes.

LANKFORD: OK.

(CROSSTALK)

COMEY: I think there's a big difference in kicking superior officers out of the Oval Office, looking the FBI director in the eye and saying, "Hope you'll let this go."

I think if our — if the agents, as good as they are, heard the president of the United States did that...

(CROSSTALK)

COMEY:... there's a real risk of a chilling effect on their work. That's why we kept it so tight.

LANKFORD: OK. OK. You had mentioned before about some news stories and news accounts, but, without having to go into all the names and the specific times and to be able dip into all that, have there been news accounts about the Russia investigation, about collusion, about this whole event or accusations that, as you read the story, you were stunned about how wrong they got the facts?

COMEY: Yes. There have been many, many stories purportedly based on classified information about — well, about lots of stuff, but especially about Russia, that are just dead wrong.

LANKFORD: I was interested in your comment that you made, as well, that the president said to you, if there were some satellite associates of his that did something wrong, it would be good to find that out.

That — the president seemed to talk to you specifically on March the 30th and say, I'm frustrated that the word is not getting out that I'm not under investigation, but if there are people that are in my circle that are, let's finish the investigation. Is that how you took it, as well?

COMEY: Yes, sir. Yes.

LANKFORD: And then you made a comment earlier about the attorney general — previous attorney general — asking you about the investigation on the Clinton e-mails, saying that you'd been asked not to call it an "investigation" anymore, but to call it a "matter."

And you had said that confused you. Can you give us additional details on that?

COMEY: Well, it concerned me, because we were at the point where we had refused to confirm the existence, as we typically do, of an investigation, for months, and it was getting to a place where that looked silly, because the campaigns were talking about interacting with the FBI in the course of our work.

The — the Clinton campaign, at the time, was using all kind of euphemisms — security review, matters, things like that, for what was going on. We were getting to a place where the attorney general and I were both going to have to testify and talk publicly about. And I wanted to know, was she going to authorize us to confirm we had an investigation?

And she said, yes, but don't call it that, call it a matter. And I said, why would I do that? And she said, just call it a matter.

And, again, you look back in hindsight, you think should I have resisted harder? I just said, all right, it isn't worth — this isn't a hill worth dying on and so I just said, OK, the press is going to completely ignore it. And that's what happened.

When I said, we have opened a matter, they all reported the FBI has an investigation open. And so that concerned me because that language tracked the way the campaign was talking about FBI's work and that's concerning.

LANKFORD: It gave the impression that the campaign was somehow using the same language as the FBI, because you were handed the campaign language and told to be able to use the campaign language...

(CROSSTALK)

COMEY: Yeah — and — and again, I don't know whether it was intentional or not, but it gave the impression that the attorney general was looking to align the way we talked about our work with the way a political campaign was describing the same activity, which was inaccurate.

We had a criminal investigation open with — as I said before, the Federal Bureau of Investigation. We had an investigation open at the time, and so that gave me a queasy feeling.

LANKFORD: Thank you.

BURR: Senator Manchin.

SENATOR JOE MANCHIN: Thank you Mr. Chairman. Thank you, Mr. Comey. I appreciate very much your being here.

West Virginia is very interested in this — in this hearing that we're having today. I've had over 600 requests for questions to ask you...

(LAUGHTER)

... from my fellow West Virginians and most of them have been asked. And there's a quite a few of them that were quite detailed that I'll ask in our classified hearing.

I want to thank you, first of all, for coming and agreeing to be here, volunteering. But also volunteering to stay into the classified hearing.

I don't know if you had a chance to watch our hearing yesterday.

COMEY: I watched part of it, yes, sir.

MANCHIN: And it was quite troubling. My colleagues here at some very pointed questions they wanted answers to. They weren't classified. They could have answered in this open setting. They refused to do so.

So that even much — makes us much more appreciative of your cooperation.

Sir, the seriousness of the Russian aggressions in our past elections and knowing that it'll be ongoing as senator King had alluded to, does — what's your concerns there? I mean, what should American public understand?

MANCHIN: People said, "Well, this is a — why are we worried about this? Why make such a big deal out of this Russian investigation?" Can you tell me what your thoughts would be?

COMEY: Yes, sir.

MANCHIN: And then the final thing is on this same topic. Did the president ever show any concern or interest or curiosity about what the Russians were doing?

COMEY: Thank you, Senator.

As I said earlier, I don't remember any conversations with the president about the Russia election interference.

MANCHIN: Did he ever ask you any questions concerning this?

COMEY: Well, there was an initial briefing of our findings, and I think there was conversation there — I don't remember it exactly — where he asked questions about what we had found and what our sources were and what our confidence level was. But after that, I don't remember anything.

The reason this is such a big deal has — we have this big, messy, wonderful country where we fight with each other all the time, but nobody tells us what to think, what to fight about, what to vote for, except other Americans, and that's wonderful and often painful.

But we're talking about a foreign government that, using technical intrusion, lots of other methods, tried to shape the way we think, we vote, we act. That is a big deal. And people need to recognize it.

It's not about Republicans or Democrats. They're coming after America, which I hope we all love equally. They want to undermine our credibility in the face of the world. They think that this great experiment of ours is a threat to them, and so they're going to try to run it down and dirty it up as much as possible.

That's what this is about. And they will be back, because we remain — as difficult as we can be with each other, we remain that shining city on the hill, and they don't like it.

(CROSSTALK)

MANCHIN: This is extremely important. It's extremely dangerous, what we're — what we're dealing with, and it's needed, is what you're saying.

COMEY: Yes, sir.

MANCHIN: Do you believe there were any tapes or recordings of your conversations with the president?

COMEY: It never occurred to me until the president's tweet. I — I'm not being facetious, I hope there are, and I'll consent to the release of them.

(CROSSTALK)

MANCHIN: So both of you — both of you are in the same findings here — you both hope there's tapes and recordings?

COMEY: Well, I mean, all I can do is hope. The president surely knows whether he taped me, and if he did, my feelings aren't hurt. Release the entire — release all the tapes, I'm good with it.

MANCHIN: Got you. Got you.

Sir, do you believe that Robert Mueller, the — our new special investigator on Russia, will be thorough and complete, without political intervention? And would you be confident on these findings and recommendations?

COMEY: Yes. Bob Mueller is one of the finest people and public servants this country's ever produced. He will do it well. He is a dogged, tough person, and you can have high confidence that, when it's done, he's turned over all the rocks.

MANCHIN: You've been asked a wide variety of — of questions today and we're going to be hearing more, I'm sure, in our classified hearing. Something I'll often ask folks when they come here — what details of this saga would be — should we be focusing on, and what would you recommend us do differently? Or to adjust our perspective on this?

COMEY: I don't know. I — and one of the reasons that I'm pleased to be here is I think this committee has shown the American people, although we have two parties and we disagree about important things, we can work together when it involves the core interests of the country.

So I would hope you'll just keep doing what you're doing. It's — it's good in and of itself, but it's also a model, especially for kids, that we — we are a functioning, adult democracy.

MANCHIN: And you also mentioned you had — I think, what, six — six meetings — three times in person, six on the phone, nine times in conversation with the president. Did he ever, at that time, allude that you were not performing adequately — ever indicate that at all?

COMEY: No. In fact, the contrary, quite often. Yeah, he called me one day. I was about to get on a helicopter, the head of the DEA was waiting in the helicopter for me, and he just called to check in and tell me I was doing an awesome job, and wanted to see how I was doing. And I said, "I'm doing fine, sir." And then I finished the call and got on the helicopter.

MANCHIN: Mr. Comey, do you believe you would have been fired if Hillary Clinton had become president?

COMEY: That's a great question. I don't know. I don't know.

MANCHIN: You have any thoughts about it?

COMEY: I might have been. I — I don't know. Look, I — I've said before, that was an extraordinarily difficult and painful time. I think I did what I had to do. I knew it was going to be very bad for me personally, and the consequences of that might have been, if Hillary Clinton was elected, I might have been terminated. I don't know. I really don't.

MANCHIN: My final question will be, after the February 14th meeting in the Oval Office, you mentioned that you asked Attorney General Sessions to ensure that you were never left alone with the president. Did you ever consider why Attorney General Sessions was not asked to stay in the room?

COMEY: Sure, I did, and — and have. And, in that moment, I...

MANCHIN: You ever talk to him about it?

COMEY: No.

MANCHIN: You never had a discussion with — with Jeff Sessions on this?

COMEY: No, not at all.

MANCHIN: On any of your meetings?

COMEY: No, I don't...

(CROSSTALK)

MANCHIN: Did he inquire — did he — did he show any inquiry whatsoever what was that meeting about?

COMEY: No. You're right, I did say to him — I'd forgotten this — when I talked to him and said, "You have to be between me and the president, and that's incredibly important," and I forget my exact words, I passed along the president's message about the importance of aggressively pursuing leaks of classified information, which is a — a goal I share.

And I passed that along to — to the attorney general, I think it was the next morning, in our — in a meeting. And — but I did not tell him about the Flynn part.

MANCHIN: Do you believe this will rise to obstruction of justice?

COMEY: I don't know. That — that's Bob Mueller's job to sort that out.

MANCHIN: Thank you, sir.

Mr. Chairman.

BURR: Senator Cotton.

SENATOR TOM COTTON: Mr. Comey, you encouraged the president to release the tapes. Will you encourage the Department of Justice or your friend at Columbia or Mr. Mueller to release your memos?

COMEY: Sure.

COTTON: You said that there — you did not record your conversations with President Obama or President Bush in memos. Did you do so with Attorney General Sessions or any other senior member of the Trump Department of Justice?

COMEY: No.

COTTON: Did you...

(CROSSTALK) COMEY: I think it — I'm sorry.

COTTON:... did you record conversations in memos with Attorney General Lynch or any other senior member of the Obama Department of Justice?

COMEY: No, not that I recall.

COTTON: In your statement for the record, you cite nine private conversations with the president, three meetings and two phone calls. There are four phone calls that are not discussed in your statement for the record. What happened in those phone calls?

COMEY: The president called me, I believe, shortly before he was inaugurated, as a follow-up to our conversation — private conversation on January the 6th. He just wanted to reiterate his rejection of the allegation and talk about — he thought about it more, and why he thought it wasn't true — the — the — the verified — unverified and salacious parts.

And — and during that call, he asked me again, "Hope you're going to stay, you're doing a great job." And I told him that I intended to. There was another phone call that I mentioned, I think was — could have the date wrong — March the 1st, where he called just to check in with me as I was about to get on the helicopter.

COMEY: There was a secure call we had about an — an operational matter that was not related to any of this, about something the FBI was working on. He wanted to make sure that I understood how important he thought it was — a totally appropriate call. And then the fourth call — I'm probably forgetting.

May have been the — I may have meant the call, when he called to invite me to dinner. I'll think about as I'm answering other questions, but I think I got that right.

COTTON: Let's turn our attention to the underlying activity at issue here: Russia's hacking into those e-mails and releasing them, and the allegations of collusion. Do you believe Donald Trump colluded with Russia?

COMEY: That's a question I don't think I should answer in an open setting. As I said, that — we didn't — that when I left, we did not have an investigation focused on President Trump. But that's a question that'll be answered by the investigation, I think.

COTTON: Let me turn to a couple of statements by one of my colleagues, Senator Feinstein. She was the ranking member on this committee until January, which means she had access to information that only she and Chairman Burr did. She's now the senior Democrat on the — on the Judiciary Committee, meaning she has access to the FBI that most of us don't.

On May 3rd, on CNN's Wolf Blitzer's show, she was asked, "Do you believe, do you have evidence that there was in fact collusion between Trump associates and Russia during the campaign?"

She answered, "Not at this time."

On May 18th, the same show, Mr. Blitzer said, "The last time we spoke, Senator, I asked if you had actually seen any evidence of collusion between the Trump campaign and the Russians, and you said to me, and I'm quoting you now — you said, 'Not at this time.' Has anything changed since we last spoke?"

Senator Feinstein said, "Well, no. No, it hasn't." Do you have any reason to doubt those statements?

COMEY: I don't doubt that Senator Feinstein was saying what — what she understood. I just don't want to go down that path, first of all, because I'm not in the government anymore, and answering in the negative, I just worry, leads me deeper and deeper into talking about the investigation in an open setting.

I don't — I — I want to be...

(CROSSTALK)

COMEY:... I'm always trying to be fair. I don't want to be unfair to President Trump. I'm not trying to suggest, by my answer, something nefarious, but I don't want to get into the business of saying not as to this person, not as to that person.

COTTON: On February 14th, the New York Times published a story, the headline of which was, "Trump Campaign Aides Had Repeated Contacts With Russian Intelligence."

You were asked earlier if that was an inaccurate story, and you said, in the main. Would it be fair to characterize that story as almost entirely wrong?

COMEY: Yes.

COTTON: Did you have, at the time that story was published, any indication of any contact between Trump people and Russians, intelligence officers, other government officials or close associates of the Russian government?

COMEY: This one, I can't answer, sitting here.

COTTON: We can discuss that in a classified setting, then.

I want to turn attention now to Mr. Flynn and the allegations of his underlying conduct: to be specific, his alleged interactions with the Russian ambassador on the telephone, and then what he said to senior Trump administration officials and Department of Justice officials.

I understand there are other issues with Mr. Flynn, related to his receipt of foreign monies or disclosure of potential advocacy activity on behalf of foreign governments. Those are serious and credible allegations that I'm sure will be pursued, but I want to speak specifically about his interactions with the Russian ambassador.

There was a story on January 23rd in the Washington Post that says — entitled, "FBI reviewed Flynn's calls with Russian ambassador but found nothing illicit." Is this story accurate?

COMEY: I don't want to comment on that, Senator, because I — I'm pretty sure the bureau has not confirmed any interception of communications. And so I don't want to talk about that in an open setting.

COTTON: Would it be improper for an incoming national security adviser to have a conversation with a foreign ambassador?

COMEY: In my — in my experience, no.

COTTON: But you can't confirm or deny that the conversation happened, and we would need to know the contents of that conversation to know if it was, in fact, improper?

COMEY: Yeah, I don't think I can talk about that in an open setting. And again, I've been out of government, now, a month, so I don't — I also don't want to talk about things when it's now somebody's — else's responsibility. But maybe in the — in the classified setting, we can talk more about that.

COTTON: You stated earlier that there wasn't an open investigation of Mr. Flynn in the FBI. Did you or any FBI agent ever sense that Mr. Flynn attempted to deceive you, or made false statements to an FBI agent?

COMEY: I don't want to go too far. That was the subject of the criminal inquiry.

COTTON: Did you ever come close to closing investigation on Mr. Flynn?

COMEY: I don't think I can talk about that in an open setting, either.

COTTON: I can discuss these more in a closed setting, then.

Mr. Comey, in — in 2004, you were a part of a well-publicized event about a intelligence program that had been recertified several times, and you were acting attorney general when Attorney General John Ashcroft was incapacitated due to illness. There was a dramatic showdown at the hospital here.

The next day, you've said that you wrote a letter of resignation, and signed it, before you — went to meet with President Bush to explain why he refused to certify it. Is that accurate?

COMEY: Yes, I think so.

COTTON: At any time in the three and half months you were the FBI director during the Trump administration, did you ever write and sign a letter of recommendation, and leave it on your desk?

COMEY: Letter of resignation? No, sir.

COTTON: Letter of resignation.

COMEY: No, sir.

COTTON: So despite all of the things that you've testified to here today, you didn't feel this rose to the level of an honest but serious difference of legal opinion between accomplished and skilled lawyers in that 2004 episode?

COMEY: I wouldn't characterize the circumstances of 2004 that way. But to answer, no, I — I didn't find — encounter any circumstance that led me to intend to resign, consider to resign. No, sir.

COTTON: Thank you.

BURR: Senator Harris.

SENATOR KAMALA HARRIS: Director Comey, I want to thank you. You are now a private citizen, and you are enduring a Senate Intelligence Committee hearing, and each of us get seven minutes instead of five, as yesterday, to ask you questions. So thank you.

COMEY: Now I'm — I'm between opportunities now, so...

HARRIS: Well, you're — you are... (LAUGHTER)

... I'm sure you'll have future opportunities.

You know, you and I are both former prosecutors. Not going to require you to answer, I just want make a statement that, in — in my — my experience of prosecuting cases, when a robber held a gun to some-body's head, and — and said, "I hope you will give me your wallet," the word "hope" was not the most operative word at that moment. But you don't have to respond to that point.

I have a series of questions to ask you, and — and they're going to start with, are you aware of any meetings between the Trump admin-istration officials and Russian officials during the campaign that have not been acknowledged by those officials in the White House?

COMEY: That's not a — even if I remember clearly, that's a not a ques-tion I can answer in an open setting.

HARRIS: Are you aware of any efforts by Trump campaign officials or associates of the campaign to hide their communications with Rus-sian officials through encrypted communications or other means?

COMEY: I have to give you same answer, Senator.

HARRIS: Sure.

In the course of the FBI's investigation, did you ever come across anything that suggested that communications, records, documents or other evidence had been destroyed?

COMEY: I think I've got to give you the same answer, because it — it would touch investigative matters.

HARRIS: And are you aware of any efforts or potential efforts to conceal communications between campaign officials and Russian of-ficials?

COMEY: I think I have to give you the same answer, Senator.

HARRIS: Thank you.

As a former attorney general, I have a series of questions about your connection with the attorney general during the course of your tenure as director. What is your understanding of the parameters of General Sessions' recusal from the Russia — Russia investigation?

COMEY: I think it's described in a written release or statement from DOJ, which I don't remember, sitting here, but the gist was he would be recused from all matters relating to Russia and the — and the campaign, or activities of Russia and the '16 election, I think. Something like that.

HARRIS: Is — so is your knowledge of the extent of his recusal based on the public statements he's made? Or the...

COMEY: Correct.

HARRIS:... OK. So was there any kind of memorandum issued from the attorney general or the Department of Justice to the FBI, outlining the parameters of his recusal?

COMEY: Not that I'm aware of.

HARRIS: And do you know if he reviewed any FBI or DOJ documents pertaining to the investigation before he was recused?

COMEY: I don't. I don't know.

HARRIS: And after he was recused, I'm assuming it's the same answer.

COMEY: Same answer.

HARRIS: And as — aside from any notice or memorandum that was not sent or was, what mechanism or processes were in place to ensure that the attorney general would not have any connection with the investigation, to your knowledge?

COMEY: I don't know for sure. I know that he had consulted with career ethics officials that know how to run a recusal at DOJ, but I don't know what mechanism they set up.

HARRIS: And the attorney general recused himself from the investigation, but do you believe it was appropriate for him to be involved in the firing of the chief investigator of that case — of that Russia interference?

COMEY: That's something I can't answer, sitting here. It — it's a reasonable question, but that would depend on a lot of things I don't know, like what did he know, what was he told, did he realize that the president was doing it because of the Russia investigation — things like that. I just don't know the answer.

HARRIS: You've mentioned in your written testimony and here that the president essentially asked you for a loyalty pledge. Are you aware of him making the same request of any other members of the Cabinet?

COMEY: I am not.

HARRIS: Do you know one way or another what he...

(CROSSTALK)

COMEY: I don't know one way or another. I never heard anything about it.

HARRIS: And you mentioned that on — you had the conversation where he hoped that you would let the Flynn matter go on February 14th or thereabouts. It's my understanding that Mr. Sessions was recused from any involvement in the investigation about a full two weeks later.

To your knowledge, was the attorney general — did he have access to information about the investigation in those interim two weeks?

COMEY: I — I don't — I — in theory, sure, because he's the attorney general. I don't know whether he had any contact with any materials related to that.

HARRIS: To your knowledge, was there any directive that he should not have any contact with any information about the Russia investigation between the February 14th date and the day he was ultimately recused — or recused himself, on March 2nd?

COMEY: Not to my knowledge. I don't know one way or another.

HARRIS: And did you speak to the attorney general about the Russia investigation before his recusal?

COMEY: I don't think so, no.

HARRIS: Do you know if anyone in the department, in the FBI, forwarded any documents or information or memos of any sort to the attention of the attorney general before his recusal?

COMEY: I don't — I don't know of any, remember any, sitting here. It's possible, but I — I don't remember any.

HARRIS: Do you know if the attorney general was involved — in fact, involved in any aspect of the Russia investigation after his recusal on the 2nd of March?

COMEY: I don't. I would assume not, but I don't — I don't — let me say it this way. I don't know of any information that would lead me to believe he did something to touch the Russia investigation after the recusal.

HARRIS: In your written testimony, you indicate that you — when you — after you were left alone with the president, you mentioned that it was inappropriate and should never happen again to the attorney general. And, apparently, he did not reply, and you write that he did not reply. What did he do, if anything? Did he just look at you? Was there a pause for a moment? What happened?

COMEY: I — I don't remember real clearly. I — I have a recollection of him just kind of looking at me — and there's a danger here I'm projecting onto him, so this may be a faulty memory — but I kind of got — his body language gave me the sense like, what am I going to do?

HARRIS: Did he shrug?

COMEY: I — I don't remember clearly. I think the reason I have that impression is I have some recollection of almost an imperceptible, like, what am I going to do? But I don't have a clear recollection of that. He didn't say anything.

HARRIS: And, on that same February 14th meeting, you said you understood the president to be requesting that you drop the investigation.

After that meeting, however, you received two calls from the president — March 30th and April 11th — where the president talked about a cloud over his presidency.

Has anything you've learned in the months since your February 14th meeting changed your understanding of the president's request? I guess it would be what he has said in public documents or public interviews?

COMEY: Correct.

HARRIS: OK. And is there anything about this investigation that you believe is in any way biased or is — is — is not being informed by a — a process of seeking the truth?

COMEY: No. The — the appointment of a special counsel should offer great — especially given who that person is — great comfort to Americans, no matter what your political affiliation is, that this will be done independently, competently and honestly.

HARRIS: And do you believe that he should have full authority, Mr. Mueller, to be able to pursue that investigation?

COMEY: Yes, and I — and, knowing him well over the years, if there's something that he thinks he needs, he will — he will speak up about it.

HARRIS: Do you believe he should have full independence?

COMEY: Yeah. And he wouldn't be part of it if he wasn't going to get full independence.

HARRIS: Thank you.

BURR: Senator Cornyn.

SENATOR JOHN CORNYN: Thank you, Mr. Chairman.

Mr. Comey, I'll repeat what I've said at previous hearings, that I believe you're a good and decent man who's been dealt a very difficult hand, starting back with the Clinton e-mail investigation. And I appreciate your willingness to appear here today voluntarily and answer our questions and cooperate with our investigation.

As a general matter, if an FBI agent has reason to believe that a crime has been committed, do they have a duty to report it?

COMEY: That's a good question. I don't know that there's a legal duty to report it. They certainly have a cultural, ethical duty to report it.

CORNYN: You're unsure whether they would have a legal duty?

COMEY: It's a good question. I've not thought about it before. I don't know where the legal — there's a statute that prohibits misprision of a felony — knowing of a felony and taking steps to conceal it — but this is a different question.

And so, look, let me be clear, I would expect any FBI agent who has reason — information about a crime being committed to report it.

CORNYN: Me, too.

COMEY: But where you rest that obligation, I don't know. It exists.

CORNYN: And let me ask you as a general proposition, if you're trying to make an investigation go away, is firing an FBI director a good way to make that happen? By that, I mean...

COMEY: Yeah.

CORNYN:... doesn't...

COMEY: It doesn't make a lot of sense to me, but I'm — I'm obviously hopelessly biased, given that I was the one fired. (LAUGHTER)

CORNYN: I understand it's personal.

COMEY: No, given the nature of the FBI, I meant what I said. There's no indispensable people in the world, including at the FBI. That — there's lots of bad things about me not being at the FBI. Most of them are for me. But the work's going to go on as before.

CORNYN: So nothing that's happened that you've testified to here today has impeded the investigation of the FBI or Director Mueller's commitment to get to the bottom of this, from the standpoint of the FBI and the Department of Justice. Would you agree with that?

COMEY: Correct, especially — the appointment of Director — Former Director Mueller is a critical part of that equation.

CORNYN: Let me take you back to the Clinton e-mail investigation. I think you've been cast as a hero or a villain depending on the — whose political ox is being gored at many different times during the course of the Clinton e-mail investigation, and even — even now, perhaps.

But you clearly were troubled by the conduct of the sitting attorney general, Loretta Lynch, when it came to the Clinton e-mail investigation. You mentioned the characterization that you'd been asked to accept that this was a "matter" and not a criminal investigation, which you've said it — it was.

There was the matter of President Clinton's meeting on the tarmac with the sitting attorney general, at a time when his wife was subject to a criminal investigation, and you've suggested that perhaps there are other matters that you may be able to share with us later on in a classified setting.

But it seems to me that you clearly believe that Loretta Lynch, the attorney general, had a — an appearance of a conflict of interest on the Clinton e-mail investigation. Is that correct?

COMEY: I think that's fair. I didn't believe she could credibly decline that investigation — at least, not without grievous damage to the Department of Justice and to the FBI.

CORNYN: And, under Department of Justice and FBI norms, wouldn't it have been appropriate for the attorney general, or, if she had recused herself — which she did not do — for the deputy attorney general to appoint a special counsel?

That's essentially what's happened now with Director Mueller. Would that have been an appropriate step in the Clinton e-mail investigation, in your opinion?

COMEY: Yes, certainly a possible step. Yes, sir.

CORNYN: And were you aware that Ms. Lynch had been requested numerous times to appoint a special counsel, and had refused?

COMEY: Yes, from — I think Congress had — members of Congress had repeatedly asked. Yes, sir.

CORNYN: Yours truly...

COMEY: OK.

CORNYN:... did on multiple occasions. And that heightened your concerns about the appearance of a conflict of interest with the Department of Justice, which caused you to make what you have described as an incredibly painful decision to basically take the matter up yourself, and — led to that July press conference.

COMEY: Yes, sir. I can — after the — President Clinton — former President Clinton met on the plane with the attorney general, I considered whether I should call for the appointment of a special counsel, and had decided that that would be an unfair thing to do, because I knew there was no case there.

We had investigated very, very thoroughly. I know this is a subject of passionate disagreement, but I knew there was no case there. And calling for the appointment of special counsel would be brutally unfair because it would send the message, aha, there's something here.

That was my judgment. Again, lots of people have different views of it. But that's how I thought about it.

CORNYN: Well, if the special counsel had been appointed, they could've made that determination that there was nothing there and declined to pursue it, right?

COMEY: Sure, but it would've been many months later, or a year later.

CORNYN: Let me just ask you to — given the experience of the Clinton e-mail investigation and what happened there, do you think it's unreasonable for anyone — any president who has been assured on multiple occasions that he's not the subject of an FBI investigation — do you think it's unreasonable for them to want the FBI director to publicly announce that, so that this cloud over his administration would be removed?

COMEY: I think that's a reasonable point of view. The concern would be, obviously, because if that boomerang comes back, it's going to be a very big deal, because there will be a duty to correct. CORNYN: Well, we — we saw that in the Clinton e-mail investigation, of course.

COMEY: Yes, I recall that.

CORNYN: I know you do. So let me ask you, finally, in the minute that we have left — there was this conversation back and forth about loyalty, and I think we all appreciate the fact that an FBI director is a unique public official in the sense that he's not — he's a political ap-pointee in one sense, but he has a duty of independence to pursue the law pursuant to the — the — the constitutional laws of the United States.

And so, when the president asked you about loyalty, you got in this back-and-forth about, well, I'll pledge you my honesty. And then it looks like, from what I've read, you agreed upon honest loyalty, or something like that. Is that the characterization?

COMEY: Yes.

CORNYN: Thank you very much.

COMEY: Thank you, sir.

BURR: Senator Reed.

SENATOR JACK REED: Thank you, Mr. Chairman. Thank you, Direc-tor Comey.

There have been press reports that the president, in addition to asking you to drop the Flynn investigation, has asked other senior intelligence officials to take steps which would tend to undermine the investigation into Russia.

There have been reports that he's asked DNI Coats and Admiral Rog-ers to make public statements exonerating him or — or taking the pressure off him, and also reports about Admiral Rogers and Director Pompeo — to intervene and reach out to the FBI and ask them.

Are you aware of any of these, or do you have any information with respect to any of these allegations?

COMEY: I don't. I'm aware of the public reporting, but I had no contact, no conversation with any of those leaders about that subject.

REED: Thank you. You have testified that you interpret the discussion with the president about Flynn as a direction to stop the investigation. Is that correct?

COMEY: Yes.

REED: You've testified that the president asked you to lift the cloud by essentially making public statement that exonerated him and perhaps others. You refused, correct?

COMEY: I didn't — I didn't do it. I didn't refuse the — the president. I told him we would see what we could do, and then the second time he called, I told him, in substance, that's something your lawyer will have to take up with the Justice Department.

REED: All right. And part of the underlying logic was that we've — we've discussed many times throughout this morning — is the duty to correct. That is one of — a theoretical issue, but also a very practical issue. It — was there — your feeling that the direction of the investigation could in fact include the president?

COMEY: Well, in theory. I mean, as I explained, the concern of one of my senior leader colleagues was, if you're looking at potential coordination between the campaign and Russia, the person at the head of the campaign is the candidate. So, logically, this person argued, the — the candidate's knowledge, understanding, will logically become a part of your inquiry if it proceeds.

And so I understood that argument. My view was that — that what I said to the president was accurate and fair, and fair to him. I resisted the idea of publicly saying it, although, if the Justice Department had wanted to, that — I would've done it, because of the duty to correct and the slippery slope problem.

REED: And, again, also, you've testified that the president asked you repeatedly to be loyal to him, and you responded you would be honestly loyal, which is, I think, your way of saying, "I'll be honest, and I'll be the head of the FBI and independent." Is that fair?

COMEY: Correct. I tried "honest" first. And also, I mean, you've — see it in my testimony — also tried to explain to him why it's in his interest, and every president's interest, for the FBI to be apart, in a way — because its credibility is important to a president and to the country.

And so I tried to hold the line, hold the line. It got very awkward, and I then said, "You'll always have honesty from me." He said, "honest loyalty," and then I acceded to that as a way to end this awkwardness.

REED: At the culmination of all these events, you're summarily fired, without any explanation or anything else?

COMEY: Well, there was an explanation. I just don't buy it.

REED: Well, yes. So you're fired. So do you believe that you were fired because you — you refused to — to take the president's direction? Is that the ultimate reason?

COMEY: I don't know for sure. I know I was fired. Again, I take the president's words. I know I was fired because of something about the way I was conducting the Russia investigation was, in some way, putting pressure on him, in some way, irritating him. And he decided to fire me because of that.

REED: Now...

COMEY: I — I can't go farther than that.

REED:... the Russian investigation, as you have pointed out, and as all my colleagues have reflected, is one of the most serious hostile acts against this country in our history.

Undermining the very core of our democracy and our elections is not a discrete event. It will likely occur — it's probably being prepared now for '18 and '20 and beyond. And yet the president of the United States fires you because, in your own words — some relation to this investigation.

And then he shows up in the Oval Office with the Russian foreign minister, first, after classifying you as crazy and a real nut job, which I think you've effectively disproved this morning. He said, "I face great pressure because of Russia. That's taken off." Your conclusion would be that the president, I would think, is downplaying the seriousness of this threat.

In fact, took specific steps to stop a thorough investigation of the Russian — Russian influence. And also, from what you've said, or what was — been said this morning, doesn't seem particularly interested in these hostile threats by the Russians? Is that fair?

COMEY: I don't know that I can agree to that level of detail. There's no doubt that it's a fair judgment — it's my judgment that I was fired because of the Russia investigation. I was fired, in some way, to change — or the endeavor was to change the way the Russia investigation was being conducted.

That is a — that is a very big deal, and not just because it involves me. The nature of the FBI and the nature of its work requires that it not be the subject of political consideration.

And on top of that you have — the Russia investigation itself is vital, because of the threat. And I know I should've said this earlier, but it's obvious — if any Americans were part of helping the Russians do that to us, that is a very big deal. And I'm confident that, if that is the case, Director Mueller will find that evidence.

REED: Finally, the president tweeted that James Comey better hope that there are no tapes of our conversation before he starts leaking to the press. Was that a rather unsubtle attempt to intimidate you from testifying, and intimidate anyone else who seriously crosses his path — of not doing it?

COMEY: I — I'm not going to sit here and try and interpret the president's tweets. It — to me, its major impact was — as I said, occurred to me in the middle of the night — holy cow, there might be tapes. And if there tapes, it's not just my word against his on — on the direction to get rid of the Flynn investigation.

REED: Thank you very much.

BURR: Senator McCain?

SENATOR JOHN MCCAIN: In the case of — Hillary Clinton, you made the statement that there wasn't sufficient evidence to bring a suit against her, although it had been very careless — in their behavior. But you did reach a conclusion in that case that it was not necessary to further pursue her.

Yet, at the same time, in the case of Mr. Trump, you said that there was not enough information to make a conclusion. Tell me the different between your conclusion as far as former Secretary Clinton is concerned and — and Mr. — Mr. Trump.

COMEY: The Clinton investigation was a completed investigation that the FBI been deeply involved in. And so I had an opportunity to understand all the facts and apply those facts against the law as I understood them. This investigation was underway, still going when I was fired. So it's nowhere near in the same place. At least, it wasn't when I was...

MCCAIN: But it's still ongoing?

COMEY:... correct, so far as I know. It was when I left.

MCCAIN: That investigation was going on. This investigation is going on. You reached separate conclusions.

COMEY: No, that one was done. The...

(CROSSTALK)

MCCAIN: That investigation of any involvement of Secretary Clinton or any of her associates is completed?

COMEY: Yes, as of July the 5th, the FBI completed its investigative work, and that's what I was announcing — what we had done and what we had found.

MCCAIN: Well, at least in the minds of this member, there's a whole lot of questions remaining about what went on, particularly considering the fact that, as you mention, it's a, quote, "big deal" as to what went on during the campaign.

So I'm glad you concluded that part of the investigation, but I — I think that the American people have a whole lot of questions out there, particularly since you just emphasized the role that Russia played.

And, obviously, she was a candidate for president at the time, so she was clearly involved in this whole situation where fake news — as you just described it, "big deal," took place. And you're going to have to help me out here. In other words, we're complete — the investigation of anything that former Secretary Clinton had to do with the campaign is over and we don't have to worry about it anymore?

COMEY: With respect to Secretary — I'm not — I'm a little confused, Senator. With respect to Secretary Clinton...

MCCAIN: Yeah.

COMEY:... we investigated criminal investigation in connection with her use of a personal e-mail server...

MCCAIN: I understand.

COMEY:... and that's the investigation I announced the conclusion of on July 5th.

MCCAIN: So — but, at the same time, you made the announcement there would be no charges brought against then Secretary Clinton for any activities involved in the Russia involvement in our — engagement in our election.

I — I don't quite understand how you could be done with that, but not complete — done with the whole investigation of their attempt to affect the outcome of our election.

COMEY: No. I'm sorry, we're not — at least, when I left — when I was fired on May the 9th, there was still an open, active investigation to understand the Russian effort, and whether any Americans work with them.

MCCAIN: But you reached the conclusion that there was no reason to bring charges again Secretary Clinton. So you reached a conclusion.

In the case of Mr. Comey, you — President Comey (sic)...

COMEY: No, sir.

MCCAIN:... I mean — excuse me — case of President Trump, you have an ongoing investigation.

So you got one candidate who you're done with and another candidate that you have a long way to go. Is that correct?

COMEY: I don't know how far the — the FBI has to go, but yes, that — the Clinton e-mail investigation was completed. The investigation of Russia's efforts in connection with the election, and whether there was any coordination, and, if so, with whom, between Russia and the campaign...

(CROSSTALK)

MCCAIN: You just made it — you just made it...

COMEY:... was ongoing when I left.

MCCAIN: You just made it clear in what you said, this is a, quote, "big deal," unquote.

I think it's hard to reconcile, in once case you reach complete conclusion, and the other side, you have — you have not, and you — in fact, obviously, there's a lot there, as — as we know — as you called it a, quote, "big deal." She's one of the candidates. But in her case, you say there will be no charges, and in the case of President Trump, there — the — the investigation continues.

MCCAIN: What has been brought out in this hearing is — is more and more emphasis on the Russian engagement and involvement in this campaign. How serious do you think this was?

COMEY: Very serious. But — I want to say some — be clear. It was — we have not announced, and there was no predication to announce, an investigation of whether the Russians may have coordinated with Secretary Clinton's campaign.

Secretary Clinton's...

(CROSSTALK)

MCCAIN:... No, but — they may not have been involved with her campaign. They were involved with the entire presidential campaign, obviously.

COMEY: Of course. Yes, sir. And that is an investigation that began last summer, and, so far as I'm aware, continues.

MCCAIN: So both President Trump and former Candidate Clinton are both involved in the investigation. Yet one of them, you said there's going to be no charges, and the other one, the — the investigation continues.

Well, I think there's a double standard there, to tell you the truth. Then, when the president said to you — you talked about the April 11th phone call, and he said, quote, "Because I've been very loyal to you, very loyal. We had that thing, you know," did that arouse your curiosity as what, quote, "that thing" was?

COMEY: Yes.

MCCAIN: Why didn't you ask him?

COMEY: It didn't seem to me to be important for the conversation we were having, to understand it. I took it to be some — an effort to — to communicate to me this — that there is a relationship between us where I've been good to you, you should be good to me.

MCCAIN: Yeah, but I — I think it would intensely arouse my curiosity if the president of the United States said "We had that thing, you know" — I'd like to know what the hell that thing is, particularly if I'm the director of the FBI.

COMEY: Yeah, I — I get that, Senator. Honestly, I'll tell you what — this is speculation, but what I concluded at the time is, in his memory, he was searching back to our encounter at the dinner, and was preparing himself to say, "I offered loyalty to you, you promised loyalty to me," and all of a sudden his memory showed him that did not happen, and I think he pulled up short.

That's just a guess, but I — I — a lot of conversations with humans over the years.

MCCAIN: I think I would have had some curiosity if it had been about me, to be honest with you. So are you aware — anything that would believe you — to believe that the president or the members of the administration or members of the campaign could potentially be used to coerce or blackmail the administration?

COMEY: That's a subject for investigations, not something I can comment on, sitting here.

MCCAIN: But you've reached that conclusion as far as Secretary Clinton was concerned. But you're not reaching a conclusion as far as this administration is concerned. Are you aware of anything that would lead you to believe that information exists that could coerce members of the administration or blackmail the administration?

COMEY: That's not a question I can answer, Senator.

BURR: Senator's time has expired.

(UNKNOWN): Thank you.

BURR: All time's expired for the hearing. Can I say, for members — we'll reconvene promptly at 1 p.m. in the hearing room. We have a vote scheduled for 1:45. I would suggest that all members promptly be there at 1 o'clock. We have about three minutes.

I'd like to have order. Photographers — photographers, return to where you were, please. This hearing's not adjourned yet. Either that, or we'll remove you.

To members, we have about three minutes of updates that we would love to cover as soon as we get into the closed session, before we have an opportunity to spend some time with Director Comey.

Based on our agreement, it would be my intentions to adjourn that closed hearing between 2 and 2:10, so that members can go vote, and I would urge you to eat at that time.

Jim, several of us on this committee have had the opportunity to work with you since you walked in the door. I want to say, personally, on behalf of all this — all the committee members, we're grateful to you for your service to your country, not just in the capacity as FBI director, but as prosecutor, and more importantly, being somebody that loves this country enough to tell it like it is.

I want to say to your workforce that we're grateful to them — with the level of cooperation that they have shown us, with the trust we've built between both organizations, the Congress and — and the bureau. We couldn't do our job if it wasn't for their willingness to share candidly with us the work that we need to see.

This hearing's the ninth public hearing this committee has had this year. That is twice the historical year-long average of this committee. I think the vice chairman and my's biggest challenge, when this investigation has concluded, is to return our hearings to the secrecy of a closed hearing, to encourage our members not to freely talk about intelligence matters publicly and to respect the fact that we have a huge job.

And that's to represent the entire body of the United States Senate and the American people, to make sure that we work with the intelligence community to provide you the tools to keep America safe, and that you do it within the legal limit, or those limits that are set by the executive branch.

We could not do it if it wasn't for a trusted partnership that you have been able to lead, and others before you. So as — as we depart from this, this is a pivotal hearing in our investigation. We're grateful to you for the professionalism you've shown, and your willingness.

I will turn to the vice chairman.

WARNER: I simply want to echo, one, again the thanks for your appearance. And there clearly still remain a number of questions.

And the one thing I want to commit to you, and more importantly, I think, Chairman, I want to commit to all those who are still potentially watching and following — there's still a lot of unanswered questions, and we're going to get to the bottom of this.

We're going to get the facts out. The American people deserve to know. There's the questions around implications of Trump officials and the Russians, but there's also the macro issue of what the Russians did and continue to do.

And I think it is very important that all Americans realize that threat is real. It is continuous. It is not just towards our nation. It is all — towards all Western democracies. And we have to come to a solution set.

Thank you, Mr. Chairman.

BURR: Director Comey, thank you once again on behalf on the committee. This hearing's adjourned.

Part Three:

Overview of the Senate Select Committee on Intelligence

Contact Information

211 Hart Senate Office Building
Washington, D.C. 20510
Phone: (202) 224-1700
Fax: (202) 224-1772

https://www.intelligence.senate.gov/

Mission

The Committee was created by the Senate in 1976 to "oversee and make
continuing studies of the intelligence activities and programs of the United
States Government," to "submit to the Senate appropriate proposals for legislation and report to the Senate concerning such intelligence activities and
programs," and to "provide vigilant legislative oversight over the intelligence
activities of the United States to assure that such activities are in conformity
with the Constitution and laws of the United States."

Composition

The Committee has 15 Senators: eight from the majority party and seven
from the minority. The one-seat majority is dictated by Senate resolution and,
unlike most other committees, does not change in proportion with the overall
Senate ratio of majority to minority membership. The Committee structure is
intended to reflect the nonpartisan nature of intelligence and encourage the
Committee to work in a bipartisan manner.

By resolution, the 15 SSCI members include two members (one per side) from
the Appropriations, Armed Services, Foreign Relations, and Judiciary Committees in order to ensure appropriate coordination with those Committees.
The Senate Majority and Minority Leaders and the Chairman and Ranking
Member of the Armed Services Committee serve as ex officio SSCI members.

Staff

The Committee's staff reviews intelligence reports, budgets, and activities;
investigates matters on behalf of the Committee; prepares legislation; and
receives briefings.

Access

While all Senators have access to classified intelligence assessments, access to intelligence sources and methods, programs, and budgets is generally limited to Intelligence Committee members (and to members of the Defense Appropriations Subcommittee). By law, the President is required to ensure that the Committee is kept "fully and currently informed" of intelligence activities—meaning that intelligence agencies are required, generally in writing, to notify the Committee of its activities and analysis. This includes keeping the Committee informed of covert actions and any significant intelligence failure.

Committee Activities

•Hearings:

The Committee meets roughly twice a week for 1 1/2 to 2 hours, generally in closed session. Most hearings involve appearances by senior Intelligence Community officials—heads of agencies, senior program managers, and senior intelligence analysts—who present testimony and answer Senators' questions. The topics for hearings include agency activities, intelligence collection programs, and intelligence analysis on a geographic region or issue (e.g., stability in the Middle East, Iran's nuclear program, terrorism threats). The Committee occasionally meets in open session, such as annual hearings to receive intelligence testimony on the national security threats to the United States, and for the Committee to consider the President's nominees to intelligence positions requiring Senate confirmation.

•Legislation:

The Committee writes an annual intelligence authorization bill that authorizes funding levels for intelligence activities (these set caps for agency funding) and provides legislative provisions that limit or allow intelligence conduct. The Committee also periodically considers stand-alone legislation, including laws governing surveillance of U.S. citizens (such as the Foreign Intelligence Surveillance Act, known as "FISA"). On occasion, the Committee reviews intelligence aspects of treaties as part of the Senate's ratification process.

•Investigations and Reviews:

The Committee conducts reviews of intelligence programs or events, ranging from routine and continuing study (the conduct of covert action programs and intelligence operations) to formal inquiries.

•Confirmations:

The Committee considers and makes recommendations to the Senate for the President's nominees to serve in intelligence positions requiring the Senate's confirmation.

•Analysis:

The Committee receives and reviews intelligence analysis on a broad range of topics to inform policy decisions.

•Daily Oversight:

The Committee, through its staff, tracks the regular collection and analysis activities of the Intelligence Community, enabling the Committee to engage with the Intelligence Community early on if it becomes aware of an issue. The Committee's Audit and Oversight staff conducts longer-term oversight projects.

James B. Comey

James B. Comey was the seventh director of the FBI, serving from September 4, 2013 under President Barak H. Obama through May 9, 2017 under President Donald J. Trump.

A Yonkers, New York native, James Comey graduated from the College of William & Mary and the University of Chicago Law School. Following law school, Comey served as an assistant United States attorney for both the Southern District of New York and the Eastern District of Virginia. Comey returned to New York to become the U.S. attorney for the Southern District of New York. In 2003, he became the deputy attorney general at the Department of Justice (DOJ).

Comey left DOJ in 2005 to serve as general counsel and senior vice president at defense contractor Lockheed Martin. Five years later, he joined Bridgewater Associates, a Connecticut-based investment fund, as its general counsel.

Notes

Notes

Notes

Notes

29311091R00068

Printed in Great Britain
by Amazon